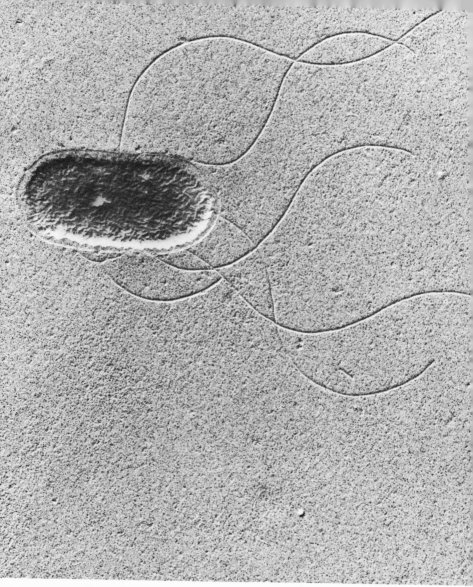

Even when magnified greatly, bacteria reveal little of their structure. This rod-shaped bacterium, magnified 30,000 times, is called Er-winia amylovora and causes a pear disease called fire blight. Several flagella, which allow the cell to move about, can be seen. SHERMAN V. THOMSON

Bacteria

HOW THEY AFFECT
OTHER LIVING THINGS

Dorothy Hinshaw Patent

HOLIDAY HOUSE · New York

PHOTO ON PAGE 74: from *Science*, Vol. 189, pp. 637-639, Fig. 1, 22 August 1975.
Copyright 1975 by the American Association for the Advancement of Science.

Library of Congress Cataloging in Publication Data
Patent, Dorothy Hinshaw.
  Bacteria, how they affect other living things.

  Bibliography: p.
  Includes index.
  SUMMARY: Describes the characteristics, functions,
and kinds of bacteria, how some keep us healthy and
others make us sick, and research done by scientists
in using bacteria to improve the quality of human life.
  1. Bacteria. [1. Bacteria] I. Title.
QR57.P369   589.9'06   79-21567
ISBN 0-8234-0401-3

For my sister, Barbara

ACKNOWLEDGMENT

I would like to thank H. Corwin Hinshaw, M.D., and Dr. Lynn Margulis for commenting on portions of my manuscript.

Contents

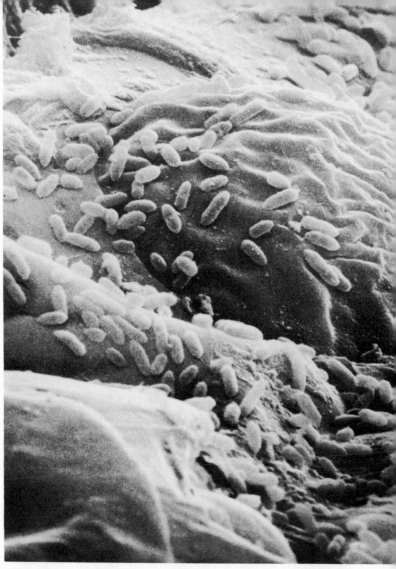

This picture of E. amylovora *was taken with a scanning electron microscope, a remarkable machine which allows us to view the microscopic world in a three-dimensional way. The bacteria are growing on the pistil of a pear flower. To us, the flower pistil is a smooth, tiny stalk inside the flower. But to the pear blight bacteria, it is a vast, bumpy surface on which to grow.* SHERMAN V. THOMSON

One

Bacteria —
Good Guys or Bad Guys?

What is the first word to pop into your mind when you hear the word "bacteria?" The chances are that your answer is "germ." Most people know of bacteria only as nasty germs that give them strep throat or food poisoning and that should be gotten rid of when at all possible.

But the vast majority of bacteria are not disease-causing germs; they are harmless or helpful organisms that we need not discourage. This is a good thing, for bacteria are so numerous almost everywhere that it would be just about impossible to eliminate them all, no matter how hard we tried. There are millions of bacteria on our skin, even after a thorough soapy shower, and the human intestine swarms with bacteria. There are countless bacteria floating about on dust particles in the air and thriving in the garden soil. Bacteria may thrive where few other living things can even survive—in boiling hot springs of Yellowstone Park; in the windswept arctic tundra; in the salty waters of the Great Salt Lake. Bacteria have been collected from ocean troughs eleven kilometers (almost seven miles) deep and from air samples taken at a height of 75 kilometers (almost 47 miles). Some bacteria can survive for many years in a dried or frozen state and "come back to life" as soon as conditions improve.

For most of human history, people have been unaware that such a thing as bacteria existed, for these organisms are much too small to be seen without a microscope. When

Anton van Leeuwenhoek made his simple but highly effective single-lens microscopes just over 300 years ago, human eyes saw bacteria for the first time. But despite the lively and informative letters which Leeuwenhoek sent to the distinguished scientists of the Royal Society of London, the further study of bacteria had to wait for another 150 years after Leeuwenhoek's death. So it is no wonder that today many aspects of bacterial life remain mysterious. These organisms exist in such amazing variety and are of such small size that studying them, especially under natural conditions, can be very difficult.

The Size of Bacteria

Bacteria are extremely small living things. While we measure our own sizes in inches or centimeters, bacterial size is measured in microns. One micron is a thousandth of a millimeter; a pinhead is about a millimeter across. Rod-shaped bacteria are usually from two to four microns long, while rounded ones are generally one micron in diameter. Thus, if you enlarged a rounded bacterium a thousand times, it would be just about the size of a pinhead. If an adult human were magnified by the same amount, he would be over a mile (1.6 kilometers) tall.

Even with an ordinary microscope, you must look closely to see bacteria. Using a magnification of 100 times, one finds that bacteria are just visible as tiny rods or dots. One cannot make out anything of their structure. Using special stains, one can see that some bacteria have attached to them wavy-looking "hairs" called flagella. Others have only one flagellum. The flagella rotate, pushing the bacteria through the water. Many bacteria lack flagella and cannot move about by their own power, while others can glide along over surfaces by some little understood mechanism.

From the bacterial point of view, the world is a very different place from what it is to humans. To a bacterium, water is as thick as molasses is to us. Bacteria are so small that they are influenced by the movements of the chemical molecules around them. Bacteria under the microscope, even those with no flagella, often bounce about in the water. This is because they collide with the water molecules and are pushed this way and that. Molecules move so rapidly that within a tenth of a second the molecules around a bacterium have all been replaced by new ones; even bacteria without flagella are thus constantly exposed to a changing environment.

Bacteria experience other habitats differently, too. To you your skin looks quite smooth, and its hairs appear very fine. But to bacteria, because of their small size, minute skin wrinkles are deep valleys and the scattered hairs are like huge tree trunks. As you read about the different kinds of bacteria and their relationships with other living things, try to keep in mind just how different the world of these minute organisms is.

Bacteria in the World

Bacteria do an incredible amount of the biochemical work on earth, processing chemicals so that they are available to other living things. Without bacteria, all life would eventually die out from lack of raw materials. Bacteria are very versatile in their ways of obtaining chemical energy. They get energy by changing (metabolizing) chemicals in their environment. Some bacteria are able to metabolize over a hundred different kinds of chemicals, while others are more limited in their abilities. Some can live without organic material, using the sun's energy in ways similar to plants. Other bacteria can survive only within the bodies of living things

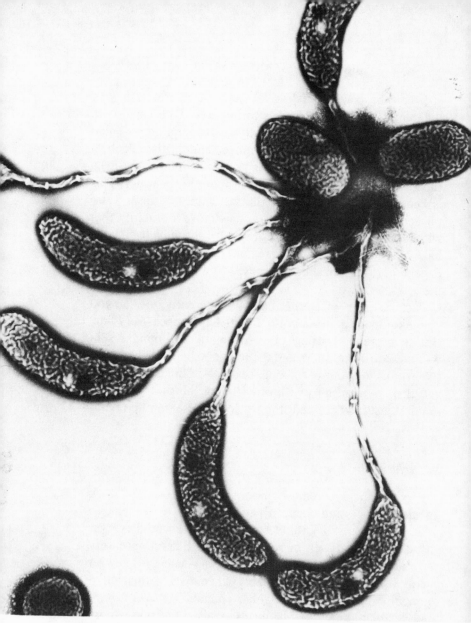

These bacteria, magnified 25,000 times, are called Caulobacter. *They are found commonly in decaying materials.* A. E. RITCHIE, NATIONAL ANIMAL DISEASE CENTER, AMES, IOWA

and need a great variety of organic materials for their survival.

Bacteria are vital in the process of decay. They help break down dead plants and animals, returning them to their basic components so that plants can recycle them again. While many bacteria help in the decay processes in the soil and on the floors of lakes and oceans, others carry out similar functions in the digestive systems of animals. Because of their biochemical versatility, bacteria are the only living things able to break down many natural chemicals. These abilities form the basis of many of their relationships with other living things.

How Bacteria "Eat"

How does a minute cell without a mouth or stomach feed itself? Bacteria absorb their nutrients directly from the environment around them. They have in them proteins called enzymes that help break down nutrient molecules and so enable the bacteria to extract energy from them. Most enzymes are quite specific and can act on only one substance or a few related substances. When bacteria are placed in a culture with one particular nutrient, the cell is stimulated to produce the enzyme that helps break down that nutrient. In this way, the cell is making only the enzymes needed at a particular time. It doesn't waste energy making enzymes that have no use at the moment.

When they are making use of some substances, bacteria must secrete the enzymes into whatever the cell is lying on or in. Materials such as cellulose exist in long, tough molecules and cannot be brought into the cell. The bacteria must attach themselves closely to the material so that, as the enzymes break it down, the resulting smaller molecules can be absorbed.

There are two main ways of getting energy out of nutrients. One way uses oxygen; the other occurs without oxygen. When the nourishing substances are metabolized where there is no oxygen, the process is called fermentation. This produces acids, which still have considerable energy locked up in them. But since organisms capable of fermenting nutrients can thrive in an oxygen-free environment, they have an advantage over those that can survive only when oxygen is available. When oxygen is present, much more energy can be extracted from nutrients. Sugars, for example, can be broken all the way down to carbon dioxide and water, releasing considerable energy along the way.

Symbiosis

Different kinds of living things are often found consistently associated with one another. Certain clown fish live among the stinging tentacles of sea anemones. Algae and fungi join forces to produce durable and hardy lichens. These are examples of symbiosis, the living together in close association of separate species. Symbiosis comes in many forms. When two species both benefit from their cooperation, it is called mutualism; if only one or neither obviously benefits, it is referred to as commensalism. Parasitism is a relationship in which one partner is injured and the other one benefits. Often it is difficult to unravel the details of such relationships, and sometimes we do not know if the symbiotic partners are harmed or aided by their association.

Bacteria often live symbiotically with other species. Some kinds are consistently found living on our skin, others in our intestines. Many bacteria can survive only within the cells of plants, and different ones inhabit animal cells. Biologists are only beginning to learn the details of some of these relationships, while others are still being discovered.

An Interconnected World

Because of the complex nature of our planet, all living things ultimately influence one another, at least indirectly. For this reason it is necessary to limit this book to some of the more obvious and intense relationships of bacteria to other living things. Many important aspects of bacterial life and many important kinds of bacteria won't be covered at all; it would take many books this size even to outline briefly all kinds of bacteria and how their activities influence other organisms.

Here you will learn about animals which cannot grow properly without their bacterial companions and about plants which can thrive in poor soil thanks to their bacterial "friends." You will see how bacteria help light up dark worlds and how they serve as important food for some rather extraordinary creatures. You will find out how some bacteria keep us healthy while others make us sick, and you'll learn of some ways in which scientists use bacteria as tools in building a better world for all people. You will also find out how, through the process of symbiosis, bacteria may have "teamed up" with one another to create the more complex cells of plants and animals. But before we go on, we'd better take a closer look at just how these minute but vital organisms are put together.

Two

The "Simplest" Cells

The variety of living things on earth is tremendous. They range in size from the smallest bacteria to huge whales and gigantic redwood trees. They may stay in one place like green plants or move around like familiar animals, and they are found in all but the harshest of the world's environments. Beneath this great diversity, however, are many similarities. All organisms are made up of individual living units called cells. Most cells are too small to be seen without a microscope, but a few can just be seen without a lens—for instance, such protozoa as paramecia, spirostoma, or amebae in a jar of water. Some organisms, like individual bacteria and protozoa, have only one cell. Others, such as elephants, have countless trillions of cells of many different types—muscle cells, nerve cells, bone cells, and so forth. But despite the variety of cell size and function, there are only two basic kinds of cells.

The simplest kind is the prokaryotic cell of bacteria. This type of cell has little visible structure, even when looked at with an electron microscope. Around the outside there is a cell wall, which gives the cell its shape. Inside the cell wall is the thin plasma membrane, which surrounds the contents of the bacterial cell. The fluid inside the cell is called the cytoplasm. This is made of water, with dissolved minerals and many other chemicals which interact in the life-maintaining processes of metabolism. Small rounded structures are scattered in the cytoplasm; these are called ribosomes. These are the protein factories of the cell.

One area in the prokaryotic cell looks different from the rest. Under the electron microscope it appears to contain fine fibers. This is called the nuclear region, and consists of a long, coiled up strand of the hereditary chemical, DNA.

More Complex Cells

The other kind of cell, called the eukaryotic cell, makes up plants and animals. It is much more complicated in structure than the prokaryotic cell. "Eu" means "true," and "karyotic" refers to the Greek word for "kernel." Thus eukaryotic cells have a true nucleus. Instead of a vague region of concentrated DNA, eukaryotic cells have a distinct compartment, separated from the rest of the cell by a definite membrane, called the nucleus.

The cytoplasm of eukaryotic cells is also more complex. It contains several different structures called organelles. Eukaryotic cells have ribosomes, but they are bigger than bacterial ones. Another kind of organelle, larger than a ribosome and found in both plant and animal cells, is called the mitochondrion. Mitochondria have complicated layers of folded membranes inside and are the powerhouses of the cell, where energy-containing chemicals are broken down to release the energy for the cell to use.

Chloroplasts are organelles found in plant cells. They are different from mitochondria, but they also contain layers of membranes. Inside the chloroplasts, water reacts with carbon dioxide, using light energy in the process; this produces sugars and oxygen. While the cytoplasm of most bacteria has little visible structure, eukaryotic cells often have complicated folds of membranes running through their cytoplasm.

Vital DNA

DNA is the key life chemical. Coded in its coils is all the information necessary for making an organism. The DNA contained within plant pollen and egg cells, or within animal sperm and ova (which are egg cells), passes the hereditary information from one generation to the next. Inside cells, the information contained in the DNA is decoded through a complicated system that directs the ribosomes to manufacture particular proteins. These proteins, such as enzymes, result eventually in the structure and function typical of the particular species.

Since bacteria are small, rather simple cells, a relatively small amount of DNA is needed to carry all the necessary genetic information. This DNA is present as one long, circular strand, somehow folded up or coiled to form the dense nuclear region of prokaryotic cells. The smallest prokaryotes contain a strand which would be about 1/4 millimeter long if stretched out, while the more complex blue-green bacteria have about three millimeters of DNA.

Eukaryotic cells, which are more complex, require larger amounts of genetic information and therefore more DNA. The simplest eukaryotic cells—yeasts—have about four and a half times as much DNA as do typical bacteria. Most eukaryotes have at least ten times as much DNA as do bacteria. This larger quantity of DNA is organized differently from bacterial DNA. Instead of being present as a single long strand, it is divided into separate chromosomes. The chromosomes can be seen as rod-shaped structures during cell division. Eukaryotic chromosomes are much more complex than the simple bacterial chromosomes. They contain certain proteins in addition to the DNA. Just exactly how the proteins and DNA are arranged in the chromosomes is not completely understood.

Classifying Life

Knowing what we know now about the differences between prokaryotic and eukaryotic cells, it is hard to understand why biologists used to think that bacteria were plants. But most of our knowledge of fine cell structure has come to us in the last 20 years or so, since the invention of the electron microscope allowed the study of cellular details. Blue-green bacteria (also called cyanobacteria) used to be considered a kind of algae, related to seaweeds and to the single-celled green algae which sometimes make aquarium water turn green. These sorts of algae all have eukaryotic nuclei and definite chloroplasts. But blue-green bacteria have folded membranes which carry on photosynthesis right in the cytoplasm; the membranes are not partitioned off into separate organelles.

Other bacteria were thought to be related to fungi, such as yeasts and mushrooms, since, like fungi, most of them cannot make their own food. But today it is clear from the structure of blue-green "algae" and bacteria that they are much more closely related to one another than to either plants or animals. Even so, many biologists still apply the name "blue-green algae" for the cyanobacteria. Since they are clearly bacteria rather than plants, this outdated name should be dropped. In this book, the terms "blue-green bacteria" and "cyanobacteria" are used for these organisms.

Biologists used to think that all living things were either plants or animals. They were divided up into two groups called kingdoms. Plants were in the kingdom Plantae and animals belonged to the kingdom Animalia. Now a third kingdom, named Monera, has been set up to cover the bacteria.

Even with three kingdoms, however, there are problems classifying life. Fungi are very different from other plants, and many scientists now place them in their own kingdom. The protozoa, or one-celled animals, have much more complicated cells than do animals with many cells. Many biologists also put the protozoa into a separate kingdom, along with some algae such as diatoms. Today more and more biologists are accepting this newer classification of living things into five kingdoms—Monera (all prokaryotes), Protista (protozoa, diatoms, and a few others), Plantae, Fungi, and Animalia.

Kinds of Bacteria

Just how to classify the bacteria themselves is a difficult problem. They have little structure to use in determining relationships. They do come in different shapes. Rod-shaped bacteria are called bacilli, or just rods, while the rounded ones are called cocci (singular, coccus). A few bacteria have variable shapes, while some are comma-shaped. Some bacteria, such as the one causing the disease syphilis, have a unique structure and spiral shape; they are called spirochaetes.

These shapes have different advantages and disadvantages. Cocci, since they have a small surface area and do not easily lose their shape when dried, are more resistant to drying than are rods. Most cocci cannot move on their own, however. It is quite difficult to propel a sphere through a liquid. Bacilli, because they have more exposed surface area, dry out more easily than cocci. But this surface area also makes it easier for them to take up nutrients from their surroundings.

Many kinds of rods have flagella and can move about. Some have only one flagellum, while others have many. Spirochaetes are usually motile, wriggling with a corkscrew-like motion. They have two sets of flagella attached near the ends of the cell. Each set extends toward the opposite end of the cell. Surrounding the whole cell, including the flagella, is an outer envelope. Just how the spirochaete flagella enable it to move is still something of a mystery.

Because these differences in shape are easy to recognize,

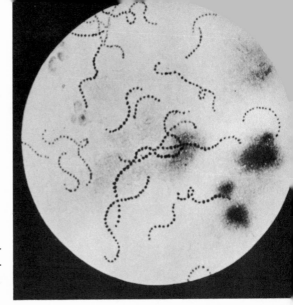

Chains of cocci (rounded bacteria) called Streptococcus pyogenes, *that cause strep throat.* HEW

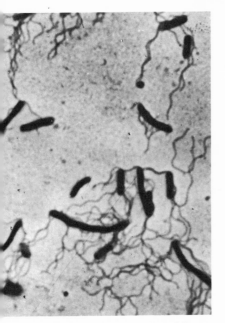

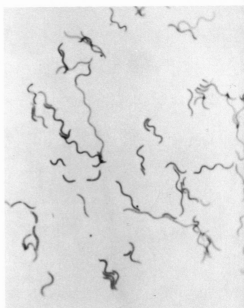

These typical rod-shaped bacteria cause the deadly disease, typhoid fever. BAUSCH AND LOMB

Spirillum is a spiral-shaped bacterium, or spirochaete. WARDS

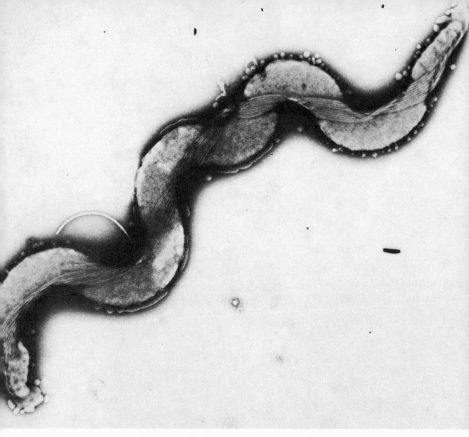

This spirochaete is magnified 44,000 times. The two sets of flagella, attached to opposite ends of the cell, can easily be seen. A. E. RIT-CHIE, NATIONAL ANIMAL DISEASE CENTER, AMES, IOWA

scientists have often classified bacteria on this basis. But when they study the metabolic activities of bacteria with different shapes, they find the same metabolic patterns in those of all three shapes. So bacteria are sometimes classified by their differences in metabolism. For example, many can survive only in the absence of oxygen; these are called anaerobic bacteria. Others require oxygen for survival; these are aerobic. Still others are more versatile, living by one sort of metabolism with oxygen present and a different kind when it is absent. To this day the classification of bacteria keeps changing, depending on whether metabolic activity, shape, or some other feature is considered most important.

Peculiar Organisms

Some bacteria have very strange characteristics. We think of living things as using organic materials for food. But many bacteria get their energy from combining oxygen with minerals. They are called lithotrophic (rock-eating) bacteria. One such, called Thiobacillus, oxidizes sulfur compounds and releases sulfuric acid. These bacteria may cause serious problems under certain circumstances. They can "feed" on minerals in bedrock shale, releasing sulfuric acid that in turn reacts with lime to form gypsum crystals. The growing gypsum crystals exert tremendous pressure (as high as 10,000 pounds per square inch), causing the rock to expand. More than 40 buildings in Pittsburg were badly damaged when the bedrock expanded under this pressure. Cleveland, Ohio, and Ottawa, Canada, have had similar problems with these bacteria. Other chemicals which some bacteria can use include hydrogen gas and iron.

A microbiologist named Dr. Richard P. Blakemore discovered some very strange bacteria in 1975. These organisms, collected from both salt- and freshwater mud in Massachusetts, always swam northward. If a magnet was brought near to them, they would change direction. Dr. Blakemore and his co-workers have studied these bacteria and found that their cells contain iron, located in numerous crystals in the cytoplasm. The crystals are not necessary for life, for bacteria grown in a medium with small amounts of iron do not develop the crystals and are not magnetic. Just what sort of advantage a tendency to be attracted to magnetic north might have for these bacteria is not known for certain. Perhaps this attraction helps keep the bacteria in the bottom mud which is their natural habitat. However, some animals that have homing abilities, and have eukaryotic cells, such as pigeons and honeybees, have deposits of magnetic materials in their bodies. Perhaps by studying these strange bacteria in detail, some hints could be gained as to whether honeybees, pigeons, and other homing animals actually might use their iron deposits to help them find their way.

The Gram Stain

However bacteria are classified, one characteristic is especially important to people interested in how bacteria interact with other living things. This feature is the Gram stain reaction, named for the Danish bacteriologist Christian Gram, who originated it. To make the Gram stain, bacteria on a slide are heated until the water around them evaporates. They are then treated with a blue dye called crystal violet. After the slide is rinsed, iodine is added in a water solution. The iodine enters the cells and reacts with the crystal violet there, producing a blue color which won't wash out with water. Up to this point, all bacteria react the same way. But now the slide is treated with a chemical, such as alcohol, which dissolves the crystal violet-iodine combination. The blue washes out of some of the cells, leaving them colorless. But it doesn't wash out of some others; they stay blue. As a final step, a red dye is used to stain the colorless cells. The bacteria which keep the blue stain are said to be "Gram-positive," while those from which the stain washed out are said to be "Gram-negative."

For a long time bacteriologists did not know why some bacteria held onto the blue stain while others lost it. They only knew that there were some basic differences between Gram-positive and Gram-negative bacteria that made the stain a useful tool. For example, most bacteria which can cause human diseases are Gram-negative, while most Gram-positive bacteria are harmless.

We now know that the differences in Gram staining are the result of important differences in cell wall structure. Gram-positive bacteria have a thick cell wall. When the cells are washed with alcohol, the water molecules in the wall are removed and the minute wall pores close up, holding in the stain. Gram-negative bacteria, however, have a thinner cell wall through which the dye can more easily be removed. Outside the cell wall, Gram-negative bacteria have another layer with a very different chemical composition. Gram-positive bacteria lack this outer layer completely.

The Gram stain isn't completely reliable. Some bacteria with a Gram positive type cell wall will give a Gram-negative staining reaction. So even this tool which helps scientists quickly distinguish between two broad groups of bacteria can be tricky. With their tremendous variety that defies easy classification, the bacteria provide many great challenges to human researchers.

Three

In Partnership with Plants

Since bacteria are so common in the air and soil around plants, you might expect that important relationships between plants and bacteria have evolved through time. Certain bacteria can cause plant diseases, but the most widespread and important relationships between these very different living things may well be the helpful ones. Some plants and bacteria help one another in only casual ways, and each can get along without the other very well. In other relationships, the partners have evolved very complicated ways of operating together that give them great advantages over their competitors or which affect their very survival.

The simplest and least studied bacteria-plant relationships concern bacteria living on leaf surfaces. Nutrients such as sugars and amino acids are given off by plant leaves, providing food for the bacteria. The microorganisms, in breaking down these chemicals to meet their own needs, produce plant hormones which make the plants grow faster. One group of scientists found 46 different strains of bacteria growing on pea leaves and stems. Twenty-six of these could produce an important plant growth hormone called IAA. Over half the bacteria isolated from corn plants were able to manufacture another important plant hormone, auxin, and this auxin appeared to be transferred from the bacteria into the corn plants themselves.

Bacteria in the Soil

The soil is truly teeming with bacteria of many different kinds. Some have no relationships at all with plants

26

and others help plants indirectly by breaking down organic material in the earth into substances which the plants can use. Many soil bacteria also make minerals such as phosphate available to plants by changing them chemically.

Soil bacteria are not evenly distributed through the ground. Near plant roots there are large numbers of some soil species. Other kinds, which may be common in the surrounding soil, are rare around roots. Bacteria are especially concentrated and active near roots. This region, where the plant has influence over the microorganisms living in the soil, is called the rhizosphere (*rhizo* means "root") and can be several millimeters thick. Like plant leaves, roots release nutrients that can be used by the surrounding bacteria. And like leaf bacteria, soil bacteria may turn these nutrients into substances that stimulate plant growth. Bacteria living within the rhizosphere of corn and wheat produce plant growth hormones and vitamins that stimulate root growth and seed germination. Corn plants cultured in sterile conditions do not grow as well as those cultured with the products of rhizosphere bacteria.

Scientists studying wheat found that bacteria around the roots changed as the plants aged, while bacteria in the nearby soil remained the same. When the plants were young, many rhizosphere bacteria could produce the plant hormone IAA from a chemical released by the roots. But as the plants grew older, these bacteria became less abundant. One puzzling fact which has come from studies such as this is that bacteria-producing chemicals which slow down plant growth are also more common near young roots. Studies of rhizosphere bacteria have only begun, and the relationships between plants and the many kinds of bacteria around their roots are very complicated. By the time other relationships, such as those with the fungi and protozoa in the soil, and the interactions among the bacteria themselves, are taken into account, the influences of living things in the soil on one another are complicated indeed.

Vital Nitrogen—the Key to Plant Growth

While most rhizosphere bacteria have received little attention until recently, certain kinds have been studied for a long time because of their immense importance to all other living things. These are the nitrogen-fixing bacteria, organisms that make the vital element nitrogen available for plant use. The air we breathe is almost 80 per cent nitrogen. But it can be used by only certain bacteria. All other living things can use nitrogen only when it is combined with other elements, such as oxygen (forming nitrite or nitrate) or hydrogen (forming ammonia). Nitrogen-fixing bacteria are therefore indispensable, for they supply the nitrogen needed by other organisms to manufacture essential proteins and other nitrogen-containing chemicals in their bodies. Without these nitrogen-fixing bacteria, the main source of available nitrogen would be cut off, and life on earth would eventually die out.

Nitrogen in the air is chemically inactive because it is firmly bound. Two nitrogen atoms are linked to one another by three strong chemical bonds which must be broken if the nitrogen is to be combined with other elements. This combined form is called N_2, or dinitrogen. When the term "nitrogen fixation" is used, it actually means "dinitrogen fixation," the combination of atmospheric dinitrogen with hydrogen taken from water molecules to produce ammonia, a chemical that is easy for plants and microorganisms to make part of their cells.

Because nitrogen-fixing bacteria are so important, scientists have studied them intensively. While plants need other elements besides nitrogen for growth, the nitrogen supply is usually the key factor concerning crop productivity. From the human point of view, the most important aspect of nitrogen fixation is the actual amount of nitrogen that plants concentrate into the edible parts, and this in turn depends on the amount of nitrogen available to them while they are growing. We do not need to depend completely on bacteria for fixed nitrogen, however; nitrogen fertilizer can be manufactured in chemical factories. About a quarter of fixed nitrogen comes from this technique, called the Haber process. But converting atmospheric nitrogen into fertilizer requires a great deal of energy and a good supply of either natural gas or petroleum to provide the necessary hydrogen. The more expensive natural gas and oil become, the more expensive manufactured fertilizer will become, and eventually the supply of fossil fuels will run out. Therefore it is very important for us to learn as much about the nitrogen-fixing bacteria as possible. Unless some other practical way of converting atmospheric nitrogen into usable substances is found, one day we will have to depend completely on these minute natural factories for our nitrogen.

Nitrogen-Fixers

The ability to fix nitrogen is strictly limited to a few kinds of bacteria, including some blue-green species. Some of these are free-living, and other exist in association with plants. While a few nitrogen-fixers can grow in the presence of oxygen, most cannot. This may seem strange, for to us oxygen is necessary for life. But oxygen can be a powerful poison which combines with all chemicals and destroys their ability to function. One chemical which oxygen destroys easily is the enzyme which enables bacteria to fix nitrogen. This enzyme is called nitrogenase. Nitrogenase from all sources is inactivated by oxygen. Once the enzyme has combined with oxygen, it is useless to the cell.

Only one group of nitrogen-fixing bacteria can actually fix nitrogen in the presence of oxygen, and these organisms devote a great deal of energy to "foiling" oxygen before it can destroy their nitrogenase. Some other nitrogen-fixers can survive in air but can fix nitrogen only when oxygen is absent, while still others can thrive only in the complete absence of oxygen. Nitrogen-fixing bacteria are most common in the ground, where often there is no oxygen. Many are scattered through the soil, but some are found living attached to the roots of plants.

Some tropical grasses have bacteria so firmly attached that vigorous washing will not remove them. Such grasses are being carefully studied for two reasons. In tropical areas there are often large numbers of poor people who need to be fed. As the price of artificial fertilizer rises, it becomes more and more difficult for poor farmers to grow good crops. Perhaps grasses with associated nitrogen-fixing bacteria could be used to enrich the soil in tropical regions, providing an inexpensive way to increase crop yields. The most important grain crops, such as corn and wheat, are also grasses. Some scientists hope that by studying the relationships between grasses and nitrogen-fixing bacteria, they can find a way to develop similar associations between crop grasses with nitrogen-fixers. If that could be done, it would have a tremendous effect on the productivity of farmlands around the world.

The Most Efficient Fixers

While free-living nitrogen-fixers make an important contribution to soil fertility, by far the most efficient ones do their job in intimate association with plants. The most familiar are between bacteria of the genus Rhizobium and plants from the legume family—peas, beans, clover, alfalfa and their relatives. Rhizobium-legume associations are responsible for about 40 per cent of all biological nitrogen fixation and for just about all the nitrogen fixed by crop plants, so they are of vital importance. By teaming up with plants, Rhizobia (the plural of Rhizobium) are able to fix more than 50 times as much nitrogen as are many free-living nitrogen-fixers, and they fix 14 times as much as the most efficient free-livers.

One reason for this greater efficiency is that the Rhizobia are comfortably housed within the roots of legumes and not actively growing while they are fixing nitrogen; the free-living bacteria are out in the soil, using most of the nitrogen they fix to manufacture their own cell components for growth. One study showed that only 7 to 13 per cent of the nitrogen fixed by free-living bacteria was excreted into the surrounding soil where it could be used by plants, while over 90 per cent of nitrogen fixed by established Rhizobia within roots went to the plant for its use.

The legume family is one of the largest plant families there is, probably the second largest in terms of numbers or individual plants. There are about 13,000 different species, ranging from small plants like peas, beans, and lupine, to bushes, small trees such as acacias, and large forest trees. Legumes are found all the way from the tropical jungle to alpine and arctic areas. Not all legumes have associations with Rhizobia, however, and many legumes have not been investigated to see if they do.

The Rhizobia associated with legumes live in special lumps on the roots called nodules. Many species of Rhizobium keep to a particular kind of legume, but some Rhizobia can form nodules on several species. Sometimes, however, even when nodules appear, they are not able to fix nitrogen. The making of nodules is a complicated process

The lumps on these soybean roots are the nodules where nitrogen-fixing bacteria live. USDA

which begins soon after the seed has sprouted and the young growing roots are probing through the soil. The roots of at least some legumes produce chemicals which attract Rhizobia to them.

Rhizobia in the soil are small flagellated rods. When the Rhizobia encounter the roots, they release chemicals which cause the microscopic root hairs to curl instead of grow straight. The surface of the root hairs appears to be coated with a particular chemical which is just right for the kind of plant, and the Rhizobia seem to have corresponding chemicals on their cell walls which can combine with the root chemicals in a "lock and key" fashion. Scientists believe that such exact and exclusive chemical interactions between the bacteria and the roots are what allow only the correct species of Rhizobium to gain entrance to the roots of the plant.

Once contact is made between the root and the bacteria, part of the root hair begins to grow inward instead of outward, forming a hollow tube called an infection thread. The infection thread, carrying an actively growing colony of Rhizobia, continues to grow back through the root hair and into the root. As it passes through root cells, they are stimulated to divide, as are nearby cells. This rapid division of cells causes the swelling which will become the nodule. Eventu-

This drawing of clover root hairs growing in culture with Rhizobia shows two hairs infected with Rhizobia and one uninfected hair in the foreground. The infection thread, growing towards the base of the hair, begins in the "kink" of the root hair. The kink is induced by the Rhizobia. Notice that the cell nuclei of the infected hairs are bigger than that of the uninfected hair. Only a small percentage of root hairs become infected. DRAWING BY THE AUTHOR

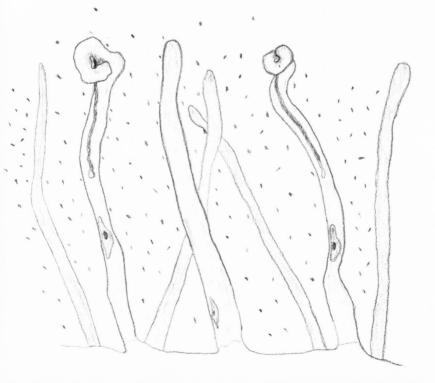

ally the infection thread breaks open, releasing bacteria into one particular kind of root cell. There the bacteria multiply until they occupy almost the entire cell. When they are through dividing, the bacteria change their shape and become "bacteroids." The bacteroids have thinner, less rigid cell walls and may be branched, forming L- and T-shaped cells.

Inside the root nodule, the bacteroids and the plant cooperate to fix nitrogen. The plant nourishes its symbionts with energy-rich chemicals manufactured through photosynthesis, and about 15 per cent of these chemicals are returned to the plant as nitrogen-containing compounds from the roots.

For many years scientists thought that Rhizobia could not fix nitrogen outside the nodules, and it was not completely clear whether they could do it all by themselves or not. But in recent years, by carefully excluding oxygen from the roots even as the plants are lifted from the soil, investigators have been able to coax Rhizobia to fix nitrogen on their own. Within the root nodule, however, bacteria are well protected from any damaging oxygen. Healthy, functioning root nodules are distinctly pink in color, because they contain a chemical unique in the plant world called leghemoglobin. This is similar to the hemoglobin found in red blood cells that carries oxygen to the cells of our bodies.

In the legume nodule, the leghemoglobin holds onto the oxygen, keeping it from poisoning the bacteria's nitrogenase. It can give up the oxygen bit by bit to the bacteria when they need it for their biological activities. The bacteria and the plant both appear to work at making the leghemoglobin, with one organism manufacturing part of the molecule and the other contributing the other portion. This mutualism between legume and Rhizobium is very valuable to both partners. The plant gives the bacteria nourishment and a safe, oxygen-free place to live, while the bacteria provide the

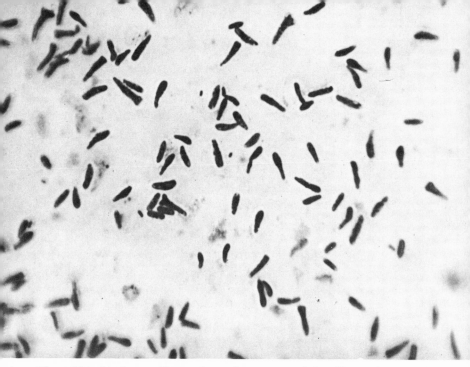

These Rhizobia bacteroids are from clover root nodules. Notice the variability of their shape, with some T-shaped cells present. USDA

plant with an abundant supply of ammonia which the plant can use for its own growth.

Other Nitrogen-Fixers

Until recently, scientists who were interested in this subtle and complicated process concentrated their attention on legumes and their Rhizobia. But we know now that some in another group of bacteria, called Actinomycetes, can make nodules on the roots of a variety of plants and fix at least as much nitrogen as do the Rhizobia. While Rhizobia (with one known exception) concentrate on legumes, Actinomycetes nodulate at least 160 plant species from seven different families. Some of these, such as the alder, are familiar trees; none are crop plants. Most live in temperate rather than tropical regions, and they are found in varied habitats. Some are bog plants, while others live on dry sand dunes. Probably because of their association with Actinomycetes, many are able to live in poor or disturbed soils along roadsides and in deserts.

Unlike most bacteria, Actinomycetes form long, branching threads of cells resembling fungus filaments. For this reason, they were long thought to be a kind of fungus. Once their prokaryotic nature was discovered, however, it was clear that they were bacteria rather than fungi. Nodule-formation by Actinomycetes has been studied in alders. As with legumes, the first visible sign of nodulation is bending of the root hairs. The growing strand of Actinomycete cells passes through the root hair. When it enters the root cells they are stimulated to divide in front of it, and the bacterial filament grows through only these long, newly divided cells. As the thread invades the root, the root cells surround it with a wall so that it is never actually in contact with the cell contents. The bacterial filaments branch and continue growing until some root cells are filled with them.

Although attempts to isolate and grow Actinomycetes which nodulate plants have been made since 1910, success did not come until 1978. The bacteria have been isolated from one kind of plant, grown in culture, and reinfected into the same kind of plant. By experimenting with different plants, scientists have found that this same species of Actinomycete can nodulate several other plants from different families. The organism grows slowly and requires at least some oxygen for growth in culture.

While legumes are very important in agriculture, the Actinomycete-nodulated plants, all of which are woody bushes or trees, are important in forestry, erosion control, and general soil improvement. Because of their ability to grow in poor soils, they might be used to help in reclaiming strip-mining land, and they can be used for improving the soil while at the same time producing a wood crop from which to make pulp. While the fixed nitrogen in the roots does not become available until the plant dies, the leaves put nitrogen back into the soil every fall when they drop from the trees. Alders add a great deal of nitrogen to the soil in this way. While most trees withdraw the valuable nitrogen-containing chemicals from their leaves before losing them in the fall, alders drop their leaves while they are still green and rich in nitrogen.

Fertilizing Rice Paddies

Rice is a vital crop over much of the earth—a staple in the diet of over half the world's people. Much rice is grown in small plots by poor farmers who cannot afford the cost of expensive factory fertilizers. Fortunately, nitrogen-fixing bacteria around the roots of rice can replace significant amounts of nitrogen. And a small water fern which grows in the paddies harbors colonies of a nitrogen-fixing blue-green bacterium which is especially efficient.

The fern, named Azolla, is a simple plant, only two to three millimeters across. It floats on top of the water and can be abundant enough to cover most of the free surface area. Azolla has cavities in its leaves which provide a home for the blue-green bacterium *Anabaena azollae.* The bacteria fix enough nitrogen for the fern, and the fern provides nutrients to the bacteria. Anabaena lives in chains of cells linked together end to end. The chains have special cells, called heterocysts, which fix nitrogen. Heterocysts have very thick walls, perhaps as an aid to keeping oxygen away from the always sensitive enzyme, nitrogenase. *Anabaena azollae* has more heterocysts than do its free-living relatives, and it is

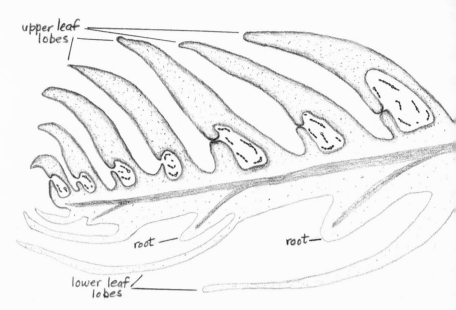

upper leaf lobes

root —

root —

lower leaf lobes

This drawing shows a leaf of the water fern Azolla, cut so that the strands of Anabaena azollae *living in the leaf cavities can be seen. Notice the fat, rounded cells scattered in the chains. These are the heterocysts, where nitrogen is fixed. The lower part of the leaf is under water, while the upper part, which carries the Anabaena, is kept above water.* DRAWING BY THE AUTHOR

able to fix more nitrogen than they do.

Azolla, with its bacterial companion, provides an excellent form of fertilizer for rice paddies. It can be grown in the off-season so that it dies and begins to decay, releasing its precious nitrogen as the rice crop grows. Or it can be grown along with the rice, preventing the growth of weeds as it enriches the paddy. Azolla has been familiar to generations of Vietnamese rice growers, some of whom guarded the secret of how to carry the ferns over the winter and provided their neighbors with fresh stock every growing season. But only in the 1970s did Western scientists begin to examine the potential of this powerful association between the simple fern and its bacterial partner.

A Mysterious Association

Some tropical shrubs and trees belonging to two plant families have symbiotic bacteria growing in fluid between the buds and in special nodules on the leaves. The bacteria are transferred from one generation to the next by infection of the seeds. But despite many years of effort by scientists trying to unravel the secrets of this association, no one knows for sure just what the plants and bacteria do for one another.

Sometimes a seed appears to escape infection and grows into a plant which develops abnormally. Such plants are called cripples. They grow slowly and have many misshapen leaves. But with time the cripples may become normal; such plants probably did actually have a few bacteria to begin with which finally became numerous enough to colonize the plants normally. Any cripples which do not become normal eventually die. Because plants completely free of bacteria are so hard to come by, experiments to determine just what the bacteria do for the plants are hard to carry out.

The bacteria isolated from some of these plants can fix nitrogen, but there is no evidence that they do so in the leaves. Plants grown in soil with little nitrogen grow poorly. If the bacteria were providing nitrogen, the plants should grow well even in nitrogen-poor soil. It is possible that the bacteria produce a plant growth substance called cytokinin, which influences the host's development. But many experiments must still be done to pin down the details of these mysterious associations.

Four

Together with
Protozoa and Insects

Vertebrate animals (those with backbones) are obvious in the world around us, largely because of their size. Who could ignore an elephant or fail to notice a camel? But by far the majority of animals fall within the group called the invertebrates—animals which lack a backbone. Worms, snails, and spiders are all invertebrates. Insects are the most familiar invertebrates, and many biologists still consider the protozoa to be members of this group. It is with these smaller but more numerous creatures that some of the most amazing examples of symbiosis with bacteria are found.

Protozoa are very small single-celled organisms which live in watery environments around the world. They are easy to find in ponds and in the sea. We have seen that many biologists today classify the protozoa separately from the animal kingdom because of their many differences from animals. But many biology textbooks still include them with the animals (the phylum name "Protozoa" means "first animals"). Most protozoans cannot be seen without the aid of a microscope. But still, they are often thousands of times larger than bacteria. Some are big enough to be seen as little specks in the water without the aid of magnification.

Like bacteria, some protozoans have flagella which enable them to move about. But the flagella of protozoa are very different from those of bacteria. They are much longer and thicker, and their structure is much more complicated. Instead of being rotated to propel the organism through the water, the flagella of eukaryotes such as protozoa are flexible and move in a wavelike fashion. Some eukaryotic cells, including many protozoa, have organelles called cilia. These have the same basic structure as flagella; they are just much shorter, and in many cases cover the protozoan rather thickly.

A great variety of protozoans contain particles now known to be symbiotic bacteria, sometimes right inside their nuclei. Some of these symbionts are completely dependent on the protozoans for survival and cannot be grown outside them. This makes them very difficult to study. But others are independent enough that they can be cultured and studied away from their hosts. One of these is a fairly typical bacterium found inside the large nucleus of a big protozoan called a spirostomum. This bacterium lacks a protective cell wall, so it is quite flexible and can take on different shapes. Similar-looking particles are found inside the nuclei of other large protozoa, so this strange partnership seems to be a quite common sort. Scientists have only begun to study these bacteria from inside cell nuclei, so no one yet knows what sort of advantage, if any, they might offer to their hosts.

The Common Paramecium and Its Guests

Paramecium aurelia is a very common protozoan, familiar to anyone who has studied microscopic life in school. Many scientists have studied aspects of paramecia in their laboratories through the years as well, and a great deal is known about their life style. Back in 1938, before the invention of the electron microscope, Dr. T. M. Sonneborn discovered a strange form in inheritance in paramecia which was associated with the cytoplasm rather than the nucleus. For many hears Dr. Sonneborn and his collegues studied the characteristics of this unusual kind of heredity. In 1948 Dr.

John R. Preer, Jr., showed that this trait, called "kappa," was associated with minute particles in the cytoplasm of paramecia. For many years kappa was considered a special and unusual particle important to studies of heredity, for it carried genetic information outside the nucleus, where all hereditary material was supposed to be. We know today that kappa is in fact a species of symbiotic bacterium rather than a natural part of the paramecium cell itself. Kappa produces shiny particles called R bodies. These are associated with a poison which kills paramecia that have no kappa. Strains of kappa exist which do not make R bodies; these are harmless. No one understands why these bacteria make this poison or whether in the natural environment the killing of other paramecia gives any advantage to strains containing kappa.

For a long time scientists argued about kappa and the other similar particles called "cytoplasmic factors" which paramecia and other protozoa contain. But today it is generally agreed that these particles are various kinds of bacteria which came from outside, rather than products of the protozoan cells themselves. The evidence for their being bacteria is quite impressive. Their sizes and shapes are similar to those of free-living bacteria, and their chemical makeup is more like that of bacteria than of protozoa. Some even possess bacterial kinds of flagella. Like bacteria, they have no mitochondria or nuclear membrane, and they usually have cell walls. Besides kappa, at least seven other kinds of cytoplasmic factors are found in *Paramecium aurelia* alone, while still another type is found in its nucleus. One Paramecium strain may have as many as five different kinds of symbionts at once.

Affecting One Another

Just what biological significance these symbionts have is still a mystery. Paramecia completely lacking symbionts live

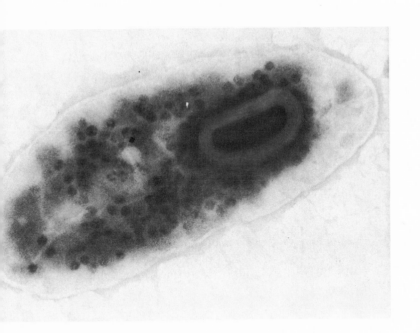

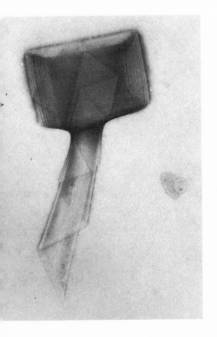

Above, kappa "particle," actually a bacterium, from Paramecium. A deadly R body can be seen inside the kappa. Somehow the unrolling of the R body, shown at left, is associated with its ability to kill paramecia.
BOTH, Journal of Cell Science, CAMBRIDGE UNIV. PRESS

perfectly healthy lives, as do those which are loaded with them. One symbiont, called lambda, may manufacture the vitamin folic acid, allowing paramecia carrying lambda particles to do without folic acid in their food. Perhaps with further study, scientists will find that other symbionts of protozoan manufacture important nutrients.

Sometimes it is possible to "cure" protozoans of their symbionts with antibiotics. The antibiotics appear not to harm the protozoans, but they are fatal to the bacteria inside.

The symbiont called lambda from Paramecium is obviously a bacterium with many flagella. Lambda may produce the vitamin folic acid for its host. Bacteriological Reviews, AMERICAN SOCIETY FOR MICROBIOLOGY

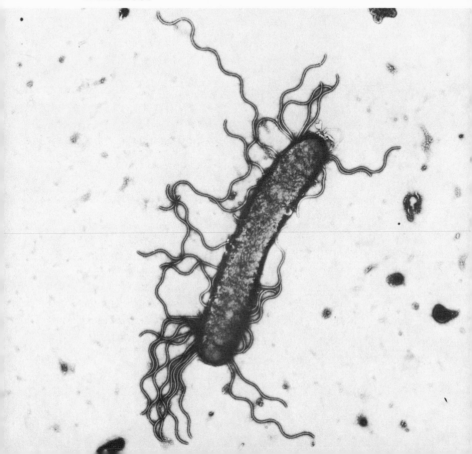

Once a "cured" strain of protozoa is available, it can be compared with the other strain to uncover differences between the two. The symbionts may prove to be vital to the protozoa. One protozoan, called Euplotes, which lives in fresh water, has from 900 to 1000 rod-shaped symbionts inside. If Euplotes is grown in penicillin, the symbionts die. Euplotes itself then stops growing and dividing to make more Euplotes. Something about the symbionts influences cell division in a vital way. If these "cured" but undividing protozoans are exposed to a culture of the symbionts, some of them become reinfected. Within five days, they begin again to grow and divide normally.

Becoming Dependent

The idea of bacteria thriving inside the cells of other living things without harming them seems strange to us, especially because we think of bacteria as "germs." But such relationships between bacteria and protozoans can develop with surprising ease. In 1966 a strain of amoeba being cultured at the University of Tennessee became infected with a kind of rod-shaped bacteria. From 60,000 to 100,000 bacteria invaded each amoeba. The amoebas were definitely sick. They grew more slowly than uninfected amoebas and starved more easily. They were also smaller. If the infected cytoplasm from the sick amoebas was injected into healthy ones, the infected animals usually died.

Fortunately the researchers, Dr. K. W. Jeon and his co-workers, did not throw out their sick cultures. They fed them and cared for them over the years and kept track of how they were doing. By 1972, the infected amobeas were growing normally, even though just as many bacteria were present in each amoeba as before. Both the amoebas and the bacteria had changed over the years. Now, if infected cytoplasm was injected into normal amoebas, they were unaffected by the bacteria; the bacteria had become apparently harmless. But if the amoebas were "cured" of the bacteria, they died. They had become dependent in some way on the bacteria. By transplanting nuclei from infected amoebas into uninfected cytoplasm, Dr. Jeon found that the nuclei could not function normally without the bacteria. Somehow, over six years, in the process of adapting to the presence of the bacteria, the amoeba nucleus had become dependent on them for normal functioning.

Digesting Blood

Mosquitoes and other bloodsuckers often have protozoans called trypanosomes living in their stomachs. Some of these trypanosomes are very dangerous to the animals that mosquitoes bite, causing malaria and related diseases, but others are harmless. Some of these protozoans have particles inside them which were originally given names like "diplosomes" and "bipolar bodies." Modern methods, such as electron microscopy, have shown that these mysterious particles are symbiotic bacteria.

The bacteria are found in limited numbers, unlike some of the symbionts of paramecia and amoebae. One mosquito protozoan has only one bacterium in its cytoplasm. Just before the protozoan divides, the bacterium divides, and one bacterial cell passes on to each new protozoan cell. If this protozoan is "cured" by the antibiotic chloroamphenicol, it can no longer grow in two kinds of nutrient solutions which used to be adequate for it. Liver extract must be added before the protozoans will grow. The symbiont provides some vital nutrients which now come from the liver extract. The same results were found with a protozoan living inside the gut of a blood-sucking bug; without its sybmionts, it also couldn't grow in certain media any more.

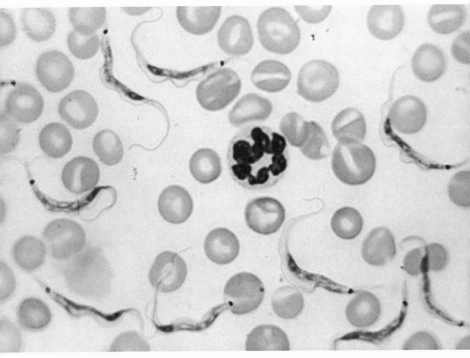

These typical trypanosomes are blood parasites. Some trypanosomes have symbiotic bacteria that probably supply important nutrients. A white blood cell can be seen near the center of the photograph. The other rounded objects are red blood cells. CAROLINA BIOLOGICAL SUPPLY CO.

Inside Insects

There is an incredible variety of symbiotic relationships between insects and bacteria, often with protozoans included along the way. Bacteria are found as symbionts in ants, beetles, bugs, cockroaches, termites, and other insects. Usually insects that have symbionts feed on a restricted diet such as wood, blood, or plant sap. The symbionts appear to provide some vital nutrients, such as vitamins, that are absent in the food. Insects such as flies and mosquitoes, which have varied diets when they are young, do not have symbionts.

They seem able to stock up on vitamins and such to use as adults. But "kissing bugs," aphids, and others which feed on one limited food all their lives, have symbionts which are vital to their health and growth.

The symbionts of closely related insects feeding on different diets are especially suited to their host's food. Bacteria from one fly which feeds on oranges are efficient at using the nitrogen and energy sources found in orange juice, while those living with a related fly are adapted to the nutrients in asparagus, the food of their host.

Some insects harbor their symbionts inside their intestines, often is special folds or pockets. Others, such as some cockroaches, have spines in their intestines to which the bacteria

Many insects with restricted diets, such as these aphids that suck plant sap, have symbiotic bacteria in their bodies. The bacteria appear to provide important nutrients to their hosts. CAROLINA BIOLOGICAL SUPPLY CO.

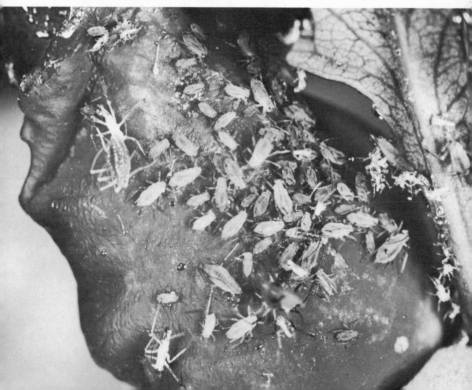

attach themselves. Many kinds, however, have evolved special organs for containing the symbionts. These are called mycetomes. This word is derived from a word for fungus, for the first insect symbionts discovered were yeasts (microscopic fungi), not bacteria, and the name "mycetome" has stuck. Within the mycetomes are specialized cells called mycetocytes, which are crammed with symbiotic bacteria.

The relationships between insects and their symbionts have evolved over a long time and are often very finely tuned. If developing cockroaches are deprived of their symbionts, the mycetomes still develop, even though they are empty. The young cockroaches are pale in color, small, and weak. Some insects need their symbionts for only part of their lives and get rid of them when they are no longer necessary. Some beetles change from wood-feeding to sucking up sap or nectar during their lives. Male beetles eliminate all the symbionts from their intestines at this time, while the females continue to carry them; thus they can be passed on to the next generation. In some insects, the males are short-lived and do not feed, and the females pass on symbionts only to their female eggs.

From One Generation to the Next

Insects pass along their symbionts in a variety of ways. When the symbionts live free in the intestine instead of within mycetocytes, they may simply be transferred by contamination. The female may deposit feces along with the eggs or may coat the eggs with symbionts from a special pouch connected to the gut. When the infant insect hatches out, it eats part of the eggshell and therefore swallows some of the vital bacteria. Insects which tend to group together, such as cockroaches or bloodsucking bugs, may simply leave transfer to chance. Since the eggs hatch in an environment already contaminated by adult insects, the young almost invariably pick up the needed symbionts.

Sometimes transfer depends on the behavior of the insects. The female of one plant-sap feeder stays near her eggs until they hatch. The hatchlings then crawl over her abdomen while she excretes droplets of liquid containing symbionts. The young suck up these droplets, thus ensuring that they will have their share of bacterial helpers.

When the bacteria live within mycetocytes, the eggs themselves may be infected with bacteria. The egg of the American cockroach is covered with a densely packed double layer of bacteria. Minute projections from the egg surface, called microvilli, extend through and over the layer of symbionts and probably help keep them near the egg. It is possible, too, that the bacteria produce some nutrients needed by the egg which are absorbed by the microvilli.

In aphids, which give birth to larvae rather than lay eggs, the early embryo becomes infected with a mass of symbiont cells which passes through a temporary pore in the outside layer of the embryo. Some sap-sucking insects have several kinds of symbionts which are passed into the egg or embryo in a mixed-up mass; later the symbionts are sorted out by type and become separated into different compartments of the mycetome.

"Curing" the Insects

The complex and intimate relationships between insects and their symbionts indicate that the bacteria are helping their hosts in vital ways. But the best way to find out just what they are doing is to study the two organisms separately. If they have become so interdependent that they cannot survive without one another, their relationship is much harder to unravel. When the eggs or young are contaminated

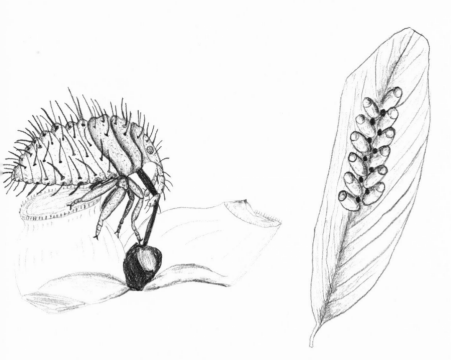

On the right is a leaf with Coptosoma eggs. The packets of symbiotic bacteria are dark masses between the eggs. On the left is a newly hatched bug sucking up the vital symbionts with its beak. DRAWING BY THE AUTHOR

externally, it is fairly easy to obtain symbiont-free insects.

The blood-sucking bug Rhodnius is easy to separate from its symbionts. The eggs can be removed right after they are laid and kept in a sterile environment. If this is done, the young insects start out developing normally. But soon they stop molting and growing, and none of them develop into adults. If they are infected with their symbiotic bacteria along the way, however, they will again resume normal development. Scientists have found that the bacteria provide vital B vitamins to the developing bugs. In other insects, too, symbionts are known to supply B vitamins missing from the diet.

The sap-sucking bug Coptosoma is also easy to free from symbionts. When the female lays her eggs, she deposits little packets of bacteria among them. When the young bugs hatch out, they head for the packets, insert their beaks into them, and suck up a supply of symbionts before heading off. If the packets are removed before the bugs hatch, the young are free of symbionts. Such bugs take a long time to develop, and only a few reach the adult stage. They lay few eggs and deposit empty packets with the eggs. In order to grow properly, Coptosoma bugs must receive their symbionts within the first 24 hours after hatching, and the bacteria must be in a special form. Bacteria from the adult or from laboratory cultures won't become helpful symbionts. Instead they invade the tissues of the host like parasites.

The Case of the Pea Aphid

We have seen that aphid symbionts are transferred directly into the developing embryos, so it is not possible to prevent infection. But different sorts of experiments have shown how the bacteria help the aphids. Pea aphids have large mycetomes lying above the gut inside the abdomen. The myceto-

These photomicrographs (photographs taken through a microscope) show the symbionts of the pea aphid. The large gray cells in A are the mycetocytes of the aphid in which the symbiotic bacteria live. They are located right next to the midgut region of the digestive system, labeled "mg." B shows an enlarged view of the mycetocytes. The nucleus (N) of one cell shows clearly, and the cytoplasm is crammed with primary symbionts. The small, dark area marked "2" is part of the sheath which contains the secondary symbionts. In C and D, the primary symbionts have been photographed through an electron microscope. Arrows show where the symbionts are dividing. Insect Science, PERGAMON PRESS LTD.

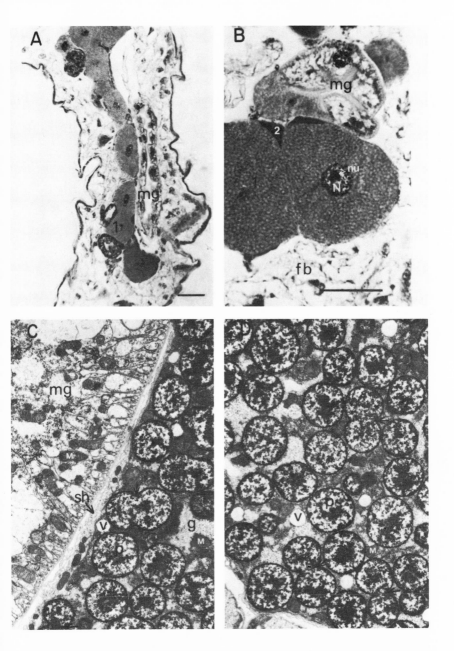

cytes are crammed with roundish primary symbionts, and the sheath surrounding the mycetocytes contains fewer rod-shaped secondary symbionts. The word "primary" implies that, during evolution, the primary symbionts were acquired by the aphids before the secondary ones.

Aphid symbionts do not divide as often as do frec-living bacteria; otherwise they would overwhelm their hosts. Now and then, the mycetocyte attacks a symbiont with enzymes which kill it and break down the cell. This process may help keep the number of symbionts manageable; it may also help release the nutrients present in the bacteria to the aphid. The cell walls of the aphid symbionts, like those of many others, are thinner than those of free-livers. Inside the protected environment of a living cell, a strong cell wall is not necessary.

The fatty substance cholesterol is necessary for life, yet insects are unable to manufacture it. Most insects can get cholesterol from their food. Aphids, however, can be raised in the laboratory on a diet completely free of the substance. In order to see if the symbionts of pea ahpids could make cholesterol and supply it to the aphids, researchers fed the aphids with the chemicals from which cholesterol is made but in this case radioactively labeled. They saw that the radioactivity first appeared within the mycetocytes, indicating that it was taken up by the symbionts. As time went by, some of the radioactivity began appearing in the tissues of the aphids. This indicated that the bacteria could make cholesterol, and that they could pass it on to their aphid hosts.

An Ancient Association

Most insects which harbor symbiotic bacteria have the sort of limited diets we've seen so far. The one glaring exception to this is found in cockroaches. These insects are among the most primitive insects, and even though most cockroaches eat a mixed diet, all kinds examined have bacteria that live in their bodies and are necessary for the insects' survival.

One especially interesting cockroach is called Cryptocercus. It lives in rotting stumps and under the bark of fallen trees. In addition to the bacteria which live inside its cells, Cryptocercus has bacteria and protozoa living in its digestive tract that are very much like those found in termites. Most termites do not have bacteria living inside their cells. But one kind from Australia does, and they look just like the ones found in cockroach cells. Since termites evolved from cockroaches about 300 million years ago, and since at least one kind of termite has the same sort of intracellular symbiont as do cockroaches, we can see that intracellular symbiosis between insects and bacteria has probably been around at least 300 million years. And since Cryptocercus has bacteria and protozoa similar to those of termites, the associations of termites with intestinal protozoa and bacteria may also be just as old.

During such a long period of time, many complex relationships could develop among the bacteria, protozoa, and termites. While scientists have studied termite protozoa pretty thoroughly, they are just beginning to look into the relationships of bacteria to both their termite hosts and to the associated protozoa. This is so despite the fact that bacteria thrive in termite guts in very large numbers; their concentration is estimated at a hundred million to ten billion cells in every milliliter of gut fluid.

The termite gut is quite complicated, but one section of it, called the paunch, is the site where most of the protozoa and bacteria live. Besides some living free in the gut fluid, bacteria may almost conpletely coat the walls of the paunch. Those that are attached have an advantage over those that

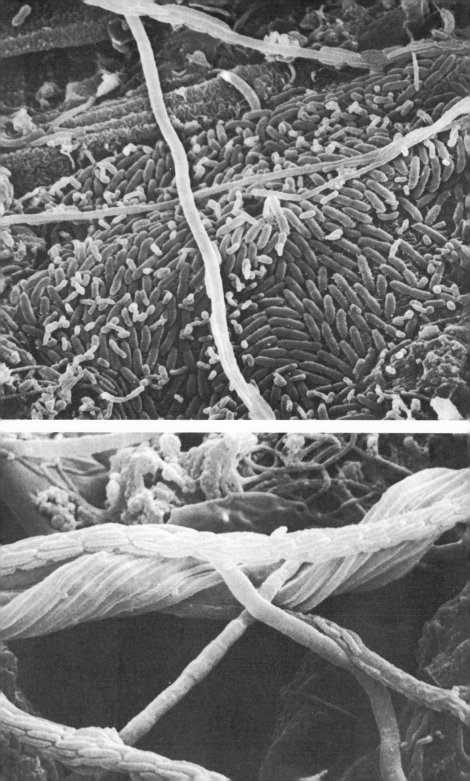

are free, for they do not risk being swept away as digested food passes on through the intestine. While some bacteria are attached to the gut walls, others are tightly glued to their larger relatives. In one American termite, thin rods were found neatly aligned in rows along the filaments of larger bacteria, sometimes almost completely covering their surface.

Bacteria are also often associated with the gut protozoa; there is a sort of symbiosis within a symbiosis. Some of the symbiotic bacteria live inside the protozoa, some in the nucleus. Others live attached to their surface. One protozoan, called Myxotricha, from an Australian termite, was originally thought to have many cilia with which it swam. But when this protozoan was looked at more closely, it was found to have only four flagella which it used for steering. The "cilia" which covered its body turned out to be spirochaetes anchored onto the protozoan by special bracket-like structures on its surface. The spirochaetes are attached to the rear surface of the brackets and move in a coordinated fashion, just as if they were really part of the protozoan, moving it steadily forward through the gut fluid. Besides serving as anchoring sites for spirochaetes, the brackets also help hold down rod-shaped bacteria which are firmly attached to the

This scanning electron micrograph (left, top) shows the very dense population of bacteria living on the surface of the termite paunch (part of the digestive system). Some kinds are attached to the surface, while others grow in long chains. DR. JOHN K. BREZNAK AND H. STUART PANKRATZ

Some chains of termite paunch bacteria have other kinds of bacteria clinging to them. Some of these chains (left, bottom) are so thickly covered by attached rods that little can be seen of the bacteria underneath. Applied and Environmental Microbiology, AMERICAN SOCIETY FOR MICROBIOLOGY

surface of Myxotricha. Bacteria of still a third kind live inside this amazing protozoan.

Other protozoans of termites have bacteria attached to them. Some spirochaetes which live on protozoa have narrow, noselike ends which contact the protozoan directly, while others have thickened, flat ends which press against the host. Neither of these two types, however, appears to help its host swim around. Some protozoa from the termitelike roach Cryptocercus are completely covered with rod-shaped bacteria attached by minute brackets. These same bacteria may be found inside the cytoplasm as well, surrounded by an envelope of plasma membrane and still held in place by the brackets. Bacteria inside protozoan cells are sometimes found only in certain regions. Some are always near the bases of the flagella, while others are found only deep inside the cell.

Whys and Wherefores

Unraveling relationships like those among the termites and their protozoan and bacterial guests can be very difficult. Three major groups of organisms are involved, and several species of protozoa and bacteria may live within one kind of termite. Termites which have protozoa rely on them to digest the cellulose in wood which they eat. If the protozoa are killed off, the termites eventually die if fed on a strict wood diet. Some biologists believe that the symbiotic bacteria give the protozoa the ability to digest cellulose, but others think the protozoa themselves can do it. All protozoa that can digest cellulose and that have been looked at so far, however, have symbiotic bacteria. The one kind found in termites which does not digest wood also doesn't have any symbiotic bacteria. Also, enzymes which can digest cellulose are commonly found in prokaryotes and rarely in eukaryotes.

Some termite gut bacteria almost certainly fulfill another important function—fixing nitrogen. We've seen that many kinds of bacteria have this ability. If termites are fed on a diet of pure cellulose, they can survive for a long time, even though cellulose contains no vital nitrogen. Termites which have their natural bacteria can fix nitrogen, and if the bacteria are killed off with antibiotics, the termites lose this ability. The protozoa in bacteria-free termites eventually die off as well, indicating that the bacteria are in some way vital to their survival.

Five

Bacteria and Digestion

Bacteria nutritionally help other organisms besides insects and protozoans; they are found in the intestines of most animals, including pigs, clams, chickens, and lobsters. A few organisms, such as some wood-boring crustaceans that live in the sea, completely lack intestinal bacteria. The absence of them in these animals is particularly surprising, for few animals are known which can produce the enzymes that break down cellulose.

Little is known about the role of bacteria in digestion in most animals, but hints that they are important abound. Bacteria live in the gut of the purple sea urchin, which feeds on algae. Every pellet of algae in the gut has a covering film of bacteria on it, and the bacteria have been cultured in the laboratory on algae. Under the microscope, it appears that the bacteria are actually digesting the algae in the pellets, but more precise studies are necessary before it can be certain that they are carrying on digestion that the sea urchins could not do on their own.

The Blood-Sucking Leech

Perhaps the animal most thoroughly dependent on bacteria for digestion is the medicinal leech, so called because it was once used widely by physicians to draw blood from patients. The leech digestive system is divided into several compartments, just like that of other animals. But the cells lining all parts of the gut are very similar, and few enzyme-secreting gland cells are to be found anywhere along its

60

length. Attempts to find leech digestive enzymes have resulted in the discovery of only a few quite slow-acting enzymes which break down proteins. No enzymes acting on fats or carbohydrates are present, and the enzymes found in other animals which split proteins into smaller pieces are not present. In the leech intestine, however, lives a single species of bacteria which possesses all the missing enzymes which the leech itself lacks. The leech takes in large quantities of blood at one feeding and may go months before feeding again. It stores the food in its crop and releases it bit by bit into the intestine. There the bacteria act on the blood, slowly breaking it down into small molecules which can be absorbed by the leech. The bacteria may also produce vitamins needed by their host. The digestive process is so well controlled that healthy-looking red blood cells may be seen in the leech gut weeks after the animal fed. If antibiotics are added to the leech's meal, the bacteria die and the leech starves on a full stomach.

Cows and Such

The digestive system of cows and their relatives is one of the most complex and highly evolved systems in all the animal world. In fact, one zoologist was so impressed with digestion in these animals that he placed them as the "top" mammals, ahead of us humans with our superior brains. Without bacteria, this amazing digestive system could not function. Cows, sheep, goats, camels, reindeer, and their relatives are called ruminants. The name comes from their habit of chewing the cud, called scientifically "rumination." Ruminants are the dominant plant-eaters on earth, due in large part to their ingenious means of digestion. These animals feed on grasses and other plant food which is low in nutritional value and hard to digest. When they eat, they tear off clumps of grass or other plants and swallow them after very little chewing. In this way, they can rapidly consume quite large amounts of food.

The food passes into the gigantic first part of the stomach, called the rumen. Actually, the rumen consists of two stomach divisions, the large rumen and the second, small compartment, called the reticulum. Since the two function as one, both may be called the rumen. It is enormous, occupying about a tenth of the animal's bulk. The cow rumen holds about 100 liters of material. The rumen itself secretes no digestive enzymes, for it is merely a container for a dense culture of dozens of species of bacteria and protozoa, an oxygen-free fermentation vat in which the plant materials are

This cross section of material from the rumen shows several different kinds of bacteria. A. E. RITCHIE, NATIONAL ANIMAL DISEASE CENTER, AMES, IOWA

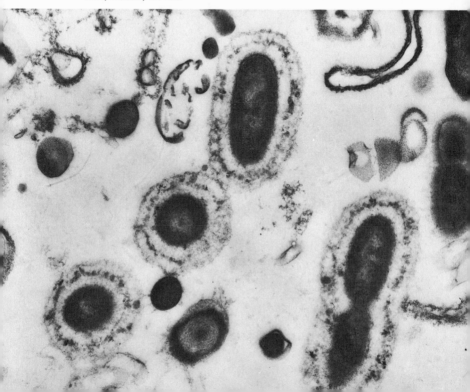

broken down into smaller organic acid molecules which the walls of the rumen absorb for use by the animal.

The bacteria and protozoa in the rumen are as dense as in the most rich and concentrated natural habitats. The environment is ideal for their growth. The temperature is warm and constant, the acidity is closely regulated, and the food is plentiful. Very little oxygen enters and what little there is is quickly disposed of by the few bacteria present which can use it. Many rumen bacteria are quite specialized. Some can attack only cellulose and related fibrous materials and must attach themselves closely to the fibers if they are to digest them. Others specialize in fermenting starch, while different species attack fats. Some of the bacteria can digest a wide variety of different chemicals but may specialize temporarily in one substance or another. Many of the protozoa can use starch or sugars, but others merely take in the abundant bacteria in their midst.

Chewing and Digesting

A ruminant spends about a third of its time eating, a third resting, and a third ruminating. Since the food is barely chewed before being swallowed, further chewing is helpful in breaking it down into smaller particles which the microbes in the rumen can more easily attack. During rumination, a mass of food is regurgitated into the mouth, and the excess fluid which accompanies it is swallowed. The cud is chewed for 30 to 60 seconds with a side-to-side grinding motion and then reswallowed. Then another mass of food is brought up for chewing. Meanwhile, in the rumen, the bacteria and protozoa are digesting the food materials continually.

Periodically, a valve at the far end of the reticulum opens and some liquid containing small particles is passed on to the next stomach compartment, called the omasum. Larger particles are held back by toothlike projections around the opening. In the omasum, water and nutrients are absorbed from the food.

From the omasum, the material passes on to the final stomach compartment, the abomasum. This is much like the true stomach of other animals. Here, stomach acids and enzymes are secreted for digestion. Digesting of what, you might ask. The bacteria and protozoa have already digested the plant materials consumed by the animals. Digestion of large numbers of protozoa and bacteria is the answer. Actually, the rumen is a huge culture chamber in which the ruminent "raises" its most important food, bacteria and protozoa. True, it absorbs some of the acid waste products of the microbes through the rumen and omasum walls, but its chief food is the microorganisms themselves. They provide the ruminant with the proteins, vitamins, and other vital materials it needs which are lacking in the plants it eats.

Special Adaptations

Ruminants have many special adaptations to their form of digestion. While the saliva of most mammals contains some digestive enzymes, that of ruminants doesn't. Cow saliva contains a great deal of sodium bicarbonate and sodium phosphate; the cow produces and swallows about 19 liters of saliva a day. The bicarbonate is needed because the rumen contents are quite acidic and become more so as the microbes digest the food. The alkaline saliva helps keep the rumen from becoming so acidic as to kill the bacteria and protozoa. In addition to organic acids, fermentation of the food produces large quantities of methane and carbon dioxide gas; the cow rumen generates 60 to 80 liters of gas a day. Thus cows must belch frequently to keep from swelling up with gas.

Young ruminants do not need their rumens as long as they

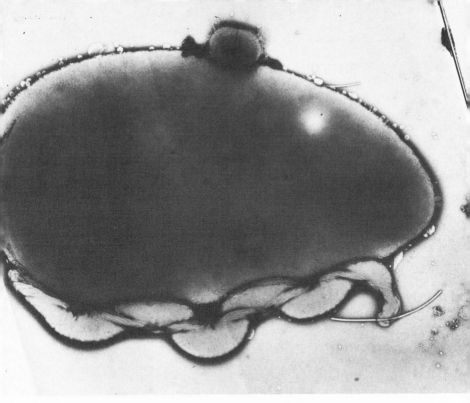

Bacteria of many sizes and shapes may live in the rumen. Here are three bacteria—a large spirochaete, a large rod, and a small rod—from the rumen of a deer. A. E. RITCHIE, NATIONAL ANIMAL DISEASE CENTER, AMES, IOWA

feed exclusively on their mother's milk. Liquid in a calf's mouth stimulates a nerve reflex which affects the stomach, causing a temporary tube to form connecting the esophagus directly with the omasum and then to the abomasum, where typical stomach digestion takes place. The abomasum of the young ruminant is proportionately larger and the rumen proportionately smaller than in the adult animal. Actual feeding on bulky material stimulates rumen development. If a calf is fed only milk, the rumen remains small. But if it is given any bulky items to eat, including inert plastic sponges, the rumen enlarges.

Other Plant-Eaters

Nonruminants that feed on plants also have special fermentation chambers where microorganisms do the work of digestion. Australian marsupials such as kangaroos, which eat plants, have very large stomachs with lots of bacteria and unique protozoa, but their stomachs are not divided into various compartments. Horses, rabbits, elephants, and some rodents have a different system. The food enters the true stomach first, where digestion begins. It then passes into the small intestine, where enzymes do their work. Only later, in the very enlarged colon and cecum, do microorganisms have an opportunity to act on the food. In the horse, the stomach has a capacity of only about 10 liters while the cecum holds 30 liters and the colon 60. This system of digestion is much less efficient than that of ruminants, for the animal has no opportunity to harvest the nutrient-rich microorganisms themselves for its own use; they pass out of the body in the feces. Rabbits and some rodents have a habit of eating their own feces. This looks like a disgusting habit to us, but it enables them to use the valuable microorganisms which grew in their intestines.

Six

Bacteria as Food

As we have seen, bacteria contribute to the diet of many insects by producing vital vitamins and other nutrients such as cholesterol and fixed nitrogen. We've also seen how bacteria, along with some protozoa, are a main portion of ruminant food. Because bacteria are just about everywhere, they end up being eaten by many organisms in an accidental way, along with their usual food. Because of their presence in or on all sorts of food, the actual importance of bacteria themselves as food is often difficult to separate from the food value of the materials they accompany.

This problem is especially difficult when dealing with animals which take in large quantities of organic matter and digest out parts of it. Earthworms, for example, eat their way through the soil, digesting what organic matter they can. Since soil is rich in bacteria, earthworms take in large quantities of them, perhaps enough to account for a significant part of their diet. Soil-dwelling bacteria capable of fixing nitrogen have been isolated from the intestines of earthworms, land snails, and cockroaches. Some biologists believe that these bacteria may be fixing nitrogen while in the intestines, increasing the food value of the materials which these animals eat.

Living on Debris

On land, the remains of dead plants return to the soil, where they are attacked by bacteria, fungi, earthworms, and other scavengers. In the sea, bits of dead seaweed float down gradually toward the bottom. Since sea water filters out light very effectively, plants thrive in only very shallow water or near the surface of deeper water. Seaweeds which live away from shore have gas-filled floats that keep them from sinking below the level where sunlight is strong. Drifting microscopic plants, and microscopic or very small animals that feed on the plants and on one another also live near the surface. This collection of living things (mostly minute but including some drifting large species) is called the plankton. Remains of plankton organisms sink gently to the bottom of the sea, along with the feces of swimming animals.

Animals of many different kinds use this "garbage" from the surface living layer of the water as food. The word "detritus" is used as a very loose term to cover such remnants which sink and eventually settle on the bottom. Detritus consists of light-weight, fluffy-looking brownish bits. While detritus looks dead, a microscope shows that it is very much alive, teeming with bacteria in the process of breaking down the detritus particles. Some protozoa and other microscopic creatures may also be there, feeding on the plant material, the bacteria, or on one another.

For many years biologists assumed that animals which feed on this detritus were digesting the materials themselves. But in recent years they have realized that the chief food of detritus-feeders is almost certainly the bacteria that are engaged in digesting the plant remains. By the time bits of plants become detritus, most of the easily digested part has already been removed by the original plant-feeders. Much of what remains is cellulose and other hard-to-digest materials. As we've seen, very few organisms other than bacteria are able to digest cellulose unaided, but bacteria are very good at it.

Clams, snails, mussels, and various worms and shrimplike crustaceans live buried in the mud or attached to rocks in shallow seaside waters. Organic material is very rich in these places, for the tide comes in and deposits particles, and the shallow water can support a good crop of algae. Laboratory experiments prove that many of these animals—mussels, some worms, tiny crustaceans, sand crabs, and some fresh-water snails and clams can all survive and grow on a diet of pure bacteria. Some organisms, in fact, grow better on bacteria alone than they do on bacteria-rich detritus.

Filtering Out Food

Many detritus-feeders have special ways of filtering out particles of particular sizes for food. Because of their small size, most bacteria pass through these filters unless they are attached to detritus or dirt particles. But small particles in rich areas such as estuaries and mud flats may be so covered with bacteria that there is a greater volume of bacteria than of the debris itself, so even animals with relatively coarse filters may feed largely on bacteria. The small marine crustacean called Corophium lives in a burrow which it rarely leaves. To feed, Corophium crawls just out of the burrow and reaches out with its front legs, dragging a clump of debris back into its burrow. It manipulates this clump with its claws in front of its mouth. Long, closely set spines called setae form a filter in front of the mouth. The water currents which the animal creates in its burrow to obtain fresh, oxygen-rich water pass across the setae and carry the finer particles of food through it to its mouth. Researchers have shown that bacteria do form an important part of Corophium's food. They fed the animals sediment to which radioactive bacteria had been added; the Corophium then became radioactive, too.

Protozoans Eat Bacteria

Bacteria are very important as protozoan food. While prokaryotes are very tiny compared to most other living things, they are relatively large objects to protozoa. Many protozoa consume various particles of different sizes, including bacteria, and quite a few appear to feed exclusively on bacteria. Sorting out the life styles of such tiny organisms can be quite a task, however, for microbial communities can be very complicated. For example, one square centimeter of fine sand and sediment in shallow water may contain individuals from 50 different species of ciliated protozoa alone, each with its own preferred little habitat and particular food requirements. Add to this the other protozoa, the bacteria, the algae, and the little multicellular animals present, and the result is one of the most complex living systems there is, about on the same level as a tropical rain forest or a teeming coral reef.

Protozoa feed on bacteria mainly by filtering them out of the water. Flagella or cilia create water currents which pull particles toward the protozoan. One kind, called Actinomonas, is attached by a thin stalk. It has one long flagellum which produces water currents passing the body. Actinomonas has long, thin extensions of its cell called pseudopodia, which it stretches out into the water currents passing by. Bacteria become stuck to the pseudopodia and are carried into the cell for digestion. Other protozoa, called choanoflagellates, have a collar surrounding the flagellum. Before the electron microscope, biologists thought the collar was solid. But now we know that it consists of very thin pseudopodia, forming a very fine filter which traps bacteria and other tiny particles as the flagellum pulls water through the collar. Trapped particles are moved down into a waiting digestive chamber, called a food vacuole, at the base of the collar.

Ciliated protozoa are the most complicated single cells known. They have parts just as specialized as those of the body of a multicellular animal. Some are completely covered with rows of cilia which beat in waves, moving them through the water. Certain rows of cilia create currents which sweep

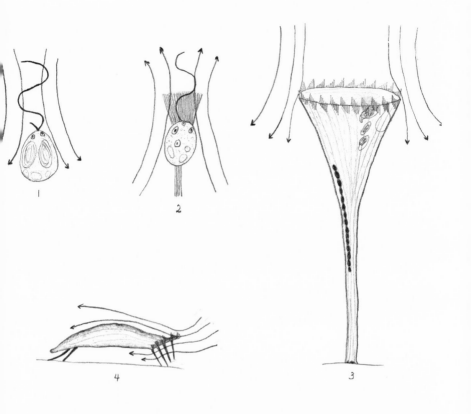

Here are four protozoans that feed on bacteria. The arrows show the direction of the water currents which bring food to the organisms. Ochromonas (1) pulls water towards itself from above, bringing bacteria which are packaged into food vacuoles near the base of the flagellum. Conaoflagellates (2) have a flagellum inside the collar which pulls bacteria in the water against the collar. The bacteria stick to the collar and are carried down the fine pseudopodia to the cell body. The large, complex ciliate Stentor (3) has rows of cilia around its funnel-shaped "body" which create currents strong enough to bring other protozoa and algae to it as well as bacteria. Euplotes (4) has clumps of fused cilia which create water currents and other clumps which act like tiny legs, allowing Euplotes to run along the surface quite rapidly. DRAWING BY THE AUTHOR

particles into a mouthlike notch, or funnel, at the bottom of which is a waiting food vacuole. After a vacuole receives some bacteria, it is pinched off and circulates slowly through the cytoplasm while digestion proceeds, and a new vacuole takes its place at the bottom of the funnel.

Some ciliates are very particular about their food. Those which live in sulfide-rich mud may feed exclusively on sulphur bacteria, perhaps even on particular kinds. Others may consume only filaments of a particular blue-green bacterium. Some of the most remarkable ciliates, called hypotrichs, often feed on bacteria. Hypotrichs look very different from most ciliates. Instead of having hairy-looking bodies covered with cilia, they have smooth, flattened bodies with little "legs." The "legs" are actually groups of fused cilia, thick and strong enough to enable the hypotrich to run along strands of algae and leaves. At the front of its body a hypotrich such as Euplotes has sets of fused cilia that beat, creating currents that draw particles into the "mouth."

Sewage Treatment

The relationships between protozoa and bacteria are of great practical importance to people, for they may form the key to successful sewage treatment. Protozoa feeding on bacteria can grow very rapidly, contributing very efficiently to the recycling of organic matter. While bacteria are necessary in the treatment of sewage, it is important that they be removed as much as possible from the water which leaves. Many kinds of protozoa, especially ciliates, live in treatment ponds and remove large numbers of bacteria from the water. If protozoa are excluded from the sewage sludge, many bacteria show up in the water leaving the pond. If ciliates are added, the number of bacteria leaving soon drops to nearly nothing.

Bacteria in sewage are important not only as potential pathogens; they can also serve as food for other pests. Blackflies are nasty insects which bite people and livestock, causing pain, swelling, and even death. Their larvae live in streams and rivers and have fine enough filters on the specialized fans around their mouths that they can grow on an exclusively bacterial diet. Blackfly outbreaks tend to occur along rivers into which sewage is dumped. Losses from them have gradually increased over the last 200 years along the heavily populated and polluted Danube River, and livestock losses have increased along the Saskatchewan River in Canada as the human population increased during this century. Because of pests like blackflies, it is vital that we come to understand as much as possible about the relationships between bacteria and their main predators, the protozoa.

Bacterial Predators

Most bacteria obtain their nourishment very passively, simply absorbing it from the surrounding medium. You can imagine the surprise of scientists when, in 1962, they discovered a small comma-shaped bacterium which is a very active predator on other bacteria. This organism, called Bdellovibrio, is different from other bacteria in several ways. Its cell wall is unique and has several ringlike structures built into the front end. Tiny fibers emerge from the rings. Bdellovibrio has an especially thick, very long flagellum which enables it to move with remarkable speed and agility. When it attacks another bacterium, Bdellovibrio dashes forth at the amazing speed of 100 cell-lengths per second. This is the equivalent of a six-foot man running a mile in fewer than nine seconds! Bdellovibrio crashes into a bacterial cell it is attacking at full tilt, shoving its prey, which is ten to 20 times its size, over a distance of several cell-lengths. After colliding, the attacker is attached to the prey cell by its specially structured front end. Somehow a minute pore is made in the cell wall of the victim, and the vibrio squeezes through it to rest between the cell wall and the plasma membrane of its host.

Once in place, the Bdellovibrio begins to grow at the expense of its victim. The host cell ceases any movement and swells up. The vibrio digests away the host cell and converts its parts into vibrio parts. It gradually grows into a long, spiral-shaped cell ten or more times larger than the original invader. After it is finished digesting away its prey, the spiral cell constricts in several places, becoming divided into several comma-shaped cells. Each cell grows a flagellum, and the new vibrios are released by the broken cell wall to go on and attack other cells.

This bacteriophage T4, a virus that attacks bacteria, is attached to the outside of a cell of the bacterium Escherichia coli. *After enzymes eat a hole in the bacterium's cell wall, the tailpiece will contract, injecting the phage DNA into the bacterial cell.* Science

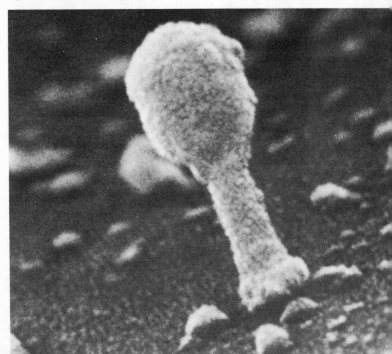

Viruses of Bacteria

Bacteria have other enemies besides predators such as ciliates, blackfly larvae, and Bdellovibrio. Viruses that are called "bacteriophages" also attack bacteria. Viruses consist of only two kinds of molecules, proteins and nucleic acids. Inside the virus is a piece of hereditary chemical which codes for the few components of the virus. Surrounding this vital core is a protective wall of protein. The structure of viruses is often so regular that they will actually crystallize, just like minerals.

Bacteriophages are quite complex viruses. A group called the "T phages" has been studied especially intensively by scientists. A T phage has a hexagonally shaped head with a tailpiece about the same length as the head. Attached to the tail is a bunch of fibers. When a T phage attacks a bacterium, the fibers attach to the cell wall of the host. Enzymes produced by the phage dissolve a hole in the cell wall. The tail contracts and injects the DNA from the head into the bacterial cell. Once inside, the phage DNA takes over the machinary of the bacterial cell, turning it into a phage factory. The bacterial ribosomes make phage proteins; the cell stops making bacterial DNA and begins to make phage DNA. The proteins and the DNA are assembled into phage particles. The infection is short but devastating. Only 20 or 30 minutes after the bacterial cell is invaded, its wall breaks open and several hundred bacteriophages are released to continue the cycle.

Seven

Glowing Bacteria

Living things which glow mysteriously have always intrigued people. Many organisms, including certain mushrooms, fish, shrimp, algae, squid, beetles, and bacteria can give off light. The search for the functions of these lights has been going on for a long time. Some cases of this "living" light—called bioluminescence—are totally mystifying to people; there seems to be no particular function for it, at least not one which the human mind can conjure up. But other kinds, as we shall see, appear to be of definite use to the glowing organisms, and often complex adaptations related to the light have evolved.

Most organisms which glow do so on their own power. Their cells, sometimes located all over the body but more often limited to certain "light organs," contain special enzyme systems which react to release light. Several kinds of bacteria are bioluminescent and are especially common in the sea. While these bacteria can generally thrive on their own in the water, they sometimes lend their light-giving power to fishes, squids, or cuttlefishes in exchange for a comfortable protected place to live.

Bacteria and Squids

We know very little so far about the relationships between luminous bacteria and their squid and cuttlefish hosts. These animals are especially difficult to keep in captivity, so studies of their lights are limited to simple observations made on shipboard right after capture and to microscopic studies of their light-organ structure.

Only a few of the many luminescent squids and cuttlefishes exploit bacteria for their lights; most glowing kinds have their own enzyme systems which produce the light. While those with their own luminescence may have bright spots scattered over their bodies or at the tips of their tentacles, those which harbor luminescent bacteria have them in a pair of organs located near the anus. The light organ has a central core containing masses of bacteria. The core is surrounded by a complex system of overlapping plates of material which form a reflector for the light. There is an outlet to the outside which contains a lenslike structure. The light organ is tucked into the wall of the ink sac, so that the only light which can be seen passes through the lens.

In some squids, the light of the light organ itself cannot be seen at all; the luminescence is visible only when fluid from the organ, containing the glowing bacteria, is released into a space called the mantle cavity or into the surrounding sea water. Just what function these light organs serve is not certain. Perhaps a squid attacked at night could emit a luminous cloud and jet away to safety while its predator stayed behind, distracted and confused by the glowing patch of water. So far, this is the most likely explanation, but until a way is devised to keep these elusive creatures in captivity or to observe them carefully at sea, we can only guess at the function of their lights.

Fish and Bacteria

Like most glowing squids, most luminescent fish glow on their own. But several different kinds do harbor bacteria in their light organs. Of the few kinds studied, the light organs seem to serve various functions for the fish. Humans, too, have even found a use for the glowing slime of one fish. Portuguese fishermen, at least in the early years of the nineteenth century, rubbed pieces of shark meat onto the belly of the glowing fish. They baited their hooks with the shining shark meat. The light lasted for hours and attracted fish to their hooks.

Some hunting fish have exploited this attraction to light, too. Water absorbs sunlight, and even at relatively shallow depths the light intensity is low. Down deeper, sunlight is totally absorbed and the depths of the sea are dark. Life in this region is sparse, for plants cannot grow. The only food for swimming creatures is other swimming creatures. Because they are so scarce, living things may only rarely come in contact with one another, so meals may be few and far between.

One group of fish, the deep-sea anglers, have several adaptations which enable them to survive in this demanding environment. The males are very small and spend most of their lives attached to the females. In that way a female is sure to have a mate once she has come in contact with one male, and the males do not compete with the females for what little food there is. The females have huge mouths with fearsome sharp teeth and can consume prey even bigger than themselves. Thus if anything resembling a meal does come along, the angler fish can make a meal of it.

Angler fish females have another important adaptation to deep-sea life, the one which gives them their name. One ray of the top fin is elongated and projects upwards in front of the fish. On the end of this strange projection is a rounded knob which may have some sort of further "decoration" extending from it. Inside the knob is a light organ that emits an alluring glow. The light organ has a structure similar to that of the squid organ. The center is filled with tubules crammed with luminescent bacteria. Around the tubules is a reflecting layer of cells which focuses the light out through the upper opening of the organ. The light, which shines towards the upper projection of the lure, presumably attracts

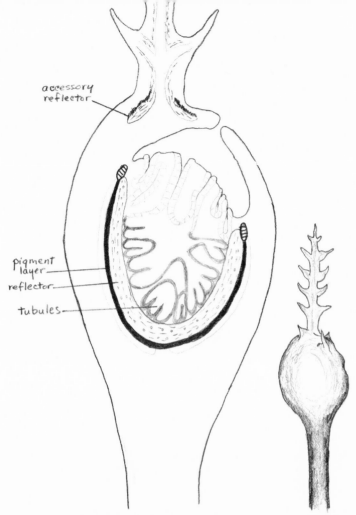

The luminescent organs of fish can be very complex. This drawing shows the "lure" of the anglerfish, Linophryne arborifera. *At the right is the lure as it looks from the outside, while on the left is a section cut through the lure to show its structure. A very dark, dense pigment layer helps contain the light. Just inside the pigment layer is the reflector, which consists of long, thin cells with crystals inside. Just inside the reflector are the tubules in which the bacteria grow. The accessory reflector in the spiny-looking projection of the lure probably helps focus some light up into the projection.* DRAWING BY THE AUTHOR

prey, which think the lure is a small glowing shrimp or fish. Once within reach of the angler, the prey has little chance of escaping its huge jaws.

Camouflaging Light

It may seem strange at first thought, but the glow from light organs probably functions as a form of camouflage for some glowing fish. Pony fish have a doughnut-shaped light organ wrapped around the esophagus, and it has an opening into the esophagus. Since luminous bacteria are common in sea water, they probably enter the light organ through this opening. But only one of the species of luminescent bacteria which can act as symbionts actually colonizes the light organ of the pony fish. The fish may be able to regulate the number of bacteria by releasing them through the opening if necessary. This light organ is found where the esophagous loops up toward the swim bladder of the fish. The swim bladder is a gas-filled organ which regulates the bouyancy of the animal. Its walls are silvery and reflect light, so it forms a natural reflector for the light organ. Translucent muscle fibers in the lower part of the body carry the light downward so that much of the lower surface of the fish has a diffuse, even glow. The bacteria emit light constantly, but the fish is able to turn the light off and on by a shutterlike mechanism so that it can glow only some of the time.

Scientists who collected pony fish for study put them into aquariums and watched them. They kept the fish in the dark and looked for light from the fish for a full 24 hours, but they stayed unlit. But when a flashlight was turned on, the fish did light up. This showed that the fish were not lighting up in order to see better or be seen at night. But why should it be useful for the fish to be lit during the daytime?

If you are a few feet under water and look upward toward the surface, you see some light filtering down into the water.

If an ordinary fish swims by above you, you will see it as a dark shape interrupting the light from above. It will be obvious and easy to see. But if the underside of that fish were lighted up, with the same shade and intensity of light as the water above, it would be very difficult to see. It would melt into its surroundings. This is just what pony fish may do— turn on their lights in the daytime, matching the intensity of the light from above so that they are "camouflaged" from the view of possible predators swimming below. No one has yet studied whether or not pony fish can actually vary the light intensity of their bodies to match that of the water above. Also, pony fish in shallow water stay near the bottom, where their lights would do no good. Their behavior in deeper water must be studied in nature to prove that these interesting fish actually do use their glowing lights as a form of camouflage.

Flashlight Fish

Angler fish appear to use bacterial light to lure their prey, and pony fish seem to use it for protection from predators. Flashlight fish, which have the most highly developed light organs of all fishes, probably use the light from their glowing bacteria for both of these functions, as well as for communication with one another. There are four known kinds of flashlight fish. Two of these, one living in the Caribbean and the other in the Gulf of California, are hardly known. But the other two kinds are common enough that scientists have been able to study them.

Flashlight fish light organs are well adapted for their function. The organ is bigger than the eye itself and lies directly beneath it. The inside surfaces are black. This protects the eyes and the internal organs from light. Inside this protective layer is a reflecting layer which directs the light outward and concentrates it. The bacteria are packed into long tubes lined with gland cells which probably provide them with nutrients.

There are as many as ten billion bacteria in each milliliter of fluid inside the tubes. Unlike the bacteria found in other fish light organs, these are not found living free in the sea water. As a matter of fact, it has so far been impossible to culture them outside the light organs. This indicates that the symbiosis between the bacteria and the flashlight fish has been around for a long time. The surface of the light organ is dotted with minute pores through which the bacteria can pass. Whether they actually do so in nature is not known.

Flashlight fish have ways of turning their lights on and off very rapidly. One kind simply rolls its organ inward so that the dark inside surface is exposed, effectively shutting off the light from the outside view. The Red Sea flashlight fish (also found in the Indian Ocean), which scientists at the Steinhardt Aquarium in San Francisco have been able to study in some detail, has an eyelidlike shutter which it can close over its "flashlight" from below. This allows it to "blink" its light very easily.

On moonlit nights and during the daytime, these fish stay in caves in the reef. But on dark nights they venture out in schools with their lights aglow. The light organs are very bright; schools of flashlight fish can easily be seen at night from the shore. Their main food consists of small shrimplike creatures which are attracted to light, so the large, glowing schools should serve as powerful beacons for their potential food. The light is bright enough, too, to make the food easily visible to the fish.

Undisturbed fish blink about three times a minute, so their lights are mainly turned on. But if the fish is alarmed, it turns off its light and darts off in an unpredictable direction. This "blink and run" tactic should be quite effective in confusing predators. One second there is a fish with bright lights ready to be eaten. Then suddenly it disappears like magic, reappearing some distance away.

In nature, mating flashlight fish defend a territory along the reef against others of their species. If an intruder shows up, the female of the pair darts back and forth excitedly. Then she douses her light and swims right up to the stranger, lowering the lid and exposing her light when she arrives. This tactic works to drive off the other fish. Scientists have also shown that the presence of other fish affects the flashlight in captivity. If a fish is exposed to another one in an adjacent tank or to a mirror placed against the side of its tank, it changes the rate of blinking. This indicates that perhaps the fish communicate with their lights even when not fighting over territories.

All in all, the flashlight fish provides one of the best examples of bioluminescence for scientists to study. The fish are relatively easy to keep in captivity, and the light organ is a very sophisticated piece of equipment. Further study of the bacteria which give the gift of light to the fish will be of interest, too, since they are from a completely new and different species which apparently cannot live outside their blinking hosts.

Why Light Up?

So far we've seen what bacterial luminescence can do for the creatures that have ways of harnessing it. But, from the bacteria's point of view, what is the use of glowing? It takes energy to produce light. Unless there is some advantage to the bacteria themselves in lighting up, there would seem to be no reason for this ability to be a trait of the bacteria in the first place. Scientists are still puzzling over this question, but one idea in particular seems promising. Except for the bacteria found in the flashlight fish, the luminescent bacteria can live perfectly well on their own. In fact, one genus of luminescent bacteria has never been found in light organs at all.

It turns out, however, that glowing bacteria can be found living inside the digestive tracts of fish and also infecting shrimps and their relatives. Although no experiments have been done so far to prove it, several scientists believe that the glowing bacteria make the shrimps more visible while infecting them. This in turn would make it easier for fish to find and eat the shrimp, so glowing bacteria would increase their chances of being eaten by fish and therefore of finding a protected home inside the fish digestive system. It would also provide an easy route for the infection of light organs of fish like the pony fish, which open right into the esophagus of the animal.

Glowing by Land

Until very recently, scientists believed that luminescent bacteria were very rare on land. But now they aren't so sure. Dr. George Poinar was studying a parasitic worm to see if it could be used to help control insect pests. The worm eats its way through the insects and kills them. When Dr. Poinar and his associate George Thomas took some dead and dying insects into the darkroom to photograph them, they were astonished to see that the insects glowed in the dark. They soon found that the light was produced by bacteria which live with the worms. As the worms develop, the bacteria also multiply. The bacteria provide some nourishment to the worms, and the worms give the bacteria a safe place to live while being transported to new insect hosts. Some caterpillars are attracted by the bacterial glow of the dead insects. The luring of new victims may be the function of luminescence, but Dr. Poinar believes further research is nesessary to confirm this.

Eight
In Us, On Us, and At Us

The countless billions of unseen bacteria which we all carry about with us wherever we go have many effects on our lives. Some of these are good effects and some are bad. The more we understand about our interactions with our microscopic fellow travelers, the better we can encourage their usefulness and discourage their harmful effects. Now and then bacteria from outside may join our usual guests and cause serious disease. Understanding these disease-causing microbes is also vitally important.

Our skin, mouths, throats, and intestines are host to amazing numbers of bacteria of many different kinds. These are called our "normal flora." Three species are found on the skin of more than 50 per cent of people, and several other kinds are also commonly found there. Van Leeuwenhoek said, "There are more animals [bacteria] living in the scum of the teeth in a man's mouth than there are men in a whole kingdom." This is true despite the fact that our mouths are constantly washed with saliva which we frequently swallow. Our noses also contain several different species, and our throats may be host to any of eight common kinds. Because of its acidity, the stomach contains only thousands of bacteria in each ounce of gastric fluid. This is a small number compared with the millions found in each ounce of saliva and the billions in every ounce of material in the large intestine. At any one time there are more bacterial cells in the large intestine than there are human cells in the entire body. Many kinds thrive there, too—one study uncovered 113 different species of bacteria living in the human large intestine.

Bacteria in the Mouth

Millions of bacteria inhabit the human mouth. If a tooth is dipped for just one minute into saliva, it becomes completely coated with a layer of firmly attached bacteria. Many mouth bacteria are able to thrive because of their ability to attach to surfaces in the mouth. Some species can attach to hard surfaces and live on teeth, while others attach best to soft tissues and live on the tongue or gums. Still other kinds do not have such efficient means of attachment and live in the cracks and crevices between the teeth and between the teeth and gums.

Even though one's mouths is often exposed to oxygen-containing air, many parts of it are anaerobic. Oxygen does not easily reach into the cracks and crevices, so anaerobic bacteria can thrive there. A layer of material, called plaque, can form on tooth surfaces. It quickly becomes anaerobic if left undisturbed. Plaque is formed by masses of bacteria held together by organic material from the bacteria and from the saliva. Shortly after a tooth is cleaned, it develops a thin coating of proteins from the saliva. Bacteria can cling to this coating very tightly, forming the beginnings of plaque. Bacterial cells make up from 60 to 70 per cent of the plaque, and if it is allowed to develop fully, the plaque may be 500 cells thick.

The different plaque bacteria may help one another. For example, one kind requires vitamin K to live and grow, and the vitamin is provided by another plaque species. If a person with plaque-covered teeth eats food high in sugar content, the sugar is turned by the anaerobic bacteria into acids which eat away the tooth enamel. This is the start of tooth decay.

Refined sugar, chemically called sucrose, can encourage decay in another way as well. One kind of decay bacteria converts sucrose into chemicals which help it anchor to the teeth, starting the formation of plaque quickly. Because plaque encourages the anaerobic bacteria which turn sugars into corroding acids, dentists nowadays encourage people to rid their teeth of plaque as much as possible every day. Use of dental floss between teeth and around the gum margin helps remove it, as does the brushing of tooth surfaces.

Normal Flora and Disease

Before the days of modern medicine and antibiotics, most serious infections were caused by disease organisms from outside the body. Tuberculosis, plague, cholera, and smallpox (caused by a virus) were the great killers of yesterday. But nowadays, because of vaccinations and antibiotic treatments, these diseases are much less important than they used to be, especially in the western world. Now, instead, more infections are caused by the normal bacteria which live with us every day. They become dangerous only under certain and rare conditions—when our bodies have lowered resistance, when they find their way to a different part of the body from where they usually live, and/or when the normal balance of bacteria has been altered. Then they may become disease-causing organisms, or pathogens.

The body's resistance to infection may be lowered in several ways. Modern drugs such as cortisone suppress the normal response of inflammation, which may be painful but which helps in fighting off disease. Radiation and drugs given for cancer therapy, and drugs given to people who receive a transplanted kidney or heart, inhibit the body's ability to attack invading microorganisms. People in hospitals, weakened by illness of one kind, may become victims of "normal" bacteria which would not harm a healthy person.

Antibiotics are wonderfully effective at helping our bodies

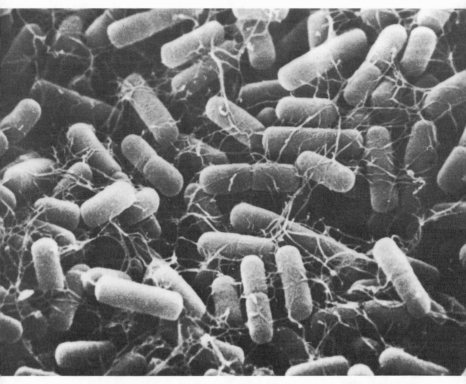

These bacteria, called Escherichia coli, *are found abundantly in human intestines. While harmless or even helpful in our intestines,* E. coli *can cause illness if it gets into a different part of the body such as the bladder.* E. coli *is the most commonly used bacterium in scientific laboratories.* PHILIPS ELECTRONIC INSTRUMENTS, INC

fight off disease. They drastically reduce the number of invading bacteria so that our natural defenses have time to develop and kill off the ones that are left. But most doctors today are careful to give them only when necessary. Antibiotics kill or inhibit all bacteria which are not resistant to them; this may include the normal flora as well as the disease organisms. This can lead to disturbances in digestion or even to serious infection by bacteria that are resistant to the antibiotic. If a resistant strain is present and the normal bacteria are killed off, the resistant strain can cause real trouble, for our normal flora help hold down the growth of dangerous bacteria in several ways. They may compete with them for nutrients, slowing their growth. They may create an environment in which disease organisms cannot grow. For example, the acidity level or oxygen content which the normal flora create may be unfavorable to the pathogen. We know that some bacteria commonly found in the throat somehow inhibit the growth of disease-causing kinds, and that normal intestinal bacteria help keep dangerous bacteria in check.

Another problem with antibiotics is that they may encourage the growth of bacteria resistant to them. When susceptible bacteria are killed off, there is less competition for any resistant bacteria which are present. In recent years scientists have discovered that bacteria of different species can exchange hereditary information, including the information for resistance to antibiotics. Normal, harmless bacteria which are drug-resistant can pass their resistance on to disease-causing bacteria from entirely different species. For this reason, doctors try to expose people to antibiotics as little as possible. If the normal flora contains resistant bacteria, they could pass this trait on to invading pathogens, making the disease difficult to treat.

"Strep Throat" and Rheumatic Fever

One infection which doctors treat promptly with antibiotics is strep throat, for this infection can lead to painful and dangerous long-term consequences. There are many kinds of bacteria called streptococci. The name comes from the Greek words for "necklace" and "berry," for streptococci can grow in long chains. Some streptococci are helpful members of our normal flora. But the species called *Streptococcus pyogenes* is the one we mean when we refer to "strep" as a disease.

Strep throat is a fairly common infection. It may lead to vomiting and high fever as well as to a painfully sore throat. When a person with a sore throat visits a doctor, the doctor may have a throat culture made if he suspects strep. If strep is found he will prescribe an antibiotic to treat it immediately. You may be surprised to learn, however, that the anitbiotic does not actually hasten recovery from this ailment. The victim may feel better soon after starting the antibiotic, but he probably would have felt just as much better without it. Then why did the doctor give the antibiotic, if it would not help the patient recover more quickly?

The reason is: to get rid of the infecting bacteria in the body as quickly as possible. If the strep organisms stay in the body more than eight days, there is danger that rheumatic fever may develop. Unfortunately, no one yet completely understands why strep leads to rheumatic fever, or why only a small percentage of the population is susceptible to it; or why rheumatic fever affects the heart in some cases, the joints in others, and the nervous system in still others. While the effects on the joints and nervous system may be alarming, it is the danger of permanent damage to the heart valves which makes doctors so eager to give antibiotics to strep victims. As long as antibiotic therapy starts by seven to eight days after the infection is felt, and the patient continues to take the antibiotic for the full ten-day treatment, rheumatic fever will not develop.

How Bacteria Cause Disease

Bacteria can cause disease in one of several ways. Some enter the body's cells and kill or damage them. Others, such as those causing cholera and diphtheria, grow outside the

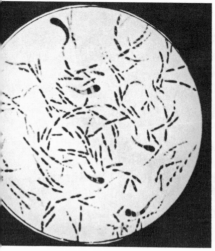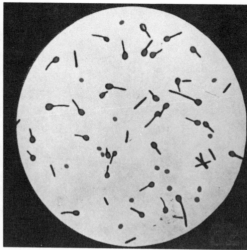

These bacteria (left) cause the often fatal disease called diphtheria. The bacteria produce poisons which kill human cells, leading to serious respiratory problems. Tetanus is caused by these bacteria (right) that can only grow when oxygen is absent. The round bodies on the slide are resistant spores that can survive for years, even if in a very dry or very cold place. If a person steps on a rusty nail which has some tetanus spores on it, the spores become activated inside the deep wound, where no oxygen can reach. They produce a powerful toxin which can cause severe muscle spasms. BOTH PHOTOS, CENTER FOR DISEASE CONTROL, HEW

cells and produce poisons, called toxins, which affect cells in one way or another, leading to disease. Still other diseases, such as food poisoning and botulism, are caused by toxins produced outside the body and then eaten with the food. The bacteria themselves do not grow inside the body.

The bacteria causing tuberculosis, called tubercle bacilli, can live and grow only inside cells. They are unusual bacteria, because their cell walls contain a great deal of fatlike material. For this reason, their cell walls repel water and therefore such water-soluble substances as acids, alkalis, and many germicides and antibiotics which can kill other bacteria. Tubercle bacilli usually enter the body from droplets in the air coughed up by an infected person. The lung is usually the first site of infection, although the bacteria are able to cause disease in just about any part of the body. The bacilli must have oxygen to live, however, and there is plenty of oxygen in the lungs.

One way the body defends itself against disease is with special cells, called macrophages, which eat up invading microorganisms and destroy them. However, tubercle bacilli are not so easily disposed of. Apparently their fatty cell walls enable them to attach rapidly to the cell membranes of macrophages and to be rapidly consumed by them—but once inside the macrophages, the bacilli do not die; they survive and grow. Not only that—they appear to stimulate the growth of more macrophages, giving themselves more places to live as they multiply.

Once enough bacteria are present, the infected area becomes inflamed. The bacteria continue to grow, and may spread to other parts of the body if the victim is not treated. The body reacts to most bacterial infections within a matter of days, producing antibodies to the invader and eliminating it. But it takes weeks for the body to control the tubercle bacilli, probably because they are living right inside the macrophages. Eventually, in most victims, the macrophages develop the ability to inhibit growth of the bacilli, and many of the bacteria are killed. The strange thing about tuberculosis, however, is that often some bacilli survive after the patient is "well." They can live for months or years inside human cells, causing no more harm. But if a person carrying these dormant bacteria around becomes run down and weakened, they may grow again and divide, causing more serious disease than they did the first time.

Tick Fevers

Tuberculosis isn't the only disease caused by bacteria living inside cells. A whole group of bacteria, called the rickettsias, have become even more dependent on cells than tubercle bacilli. For many years, scientists weren't even sure if rickettsias were bacteria. They are much smaller than most bacteria, but they are bigger than viruses. The modern electron microscope, however, makes it clear that these tiny parasites are truly bacteria. Rickettsias live inside the cells of lice, ticks, and fleas. Usually they do not harm these hosts. But some rickettsias, if transferred to a human, can cause fatal diseases. Epidemic typhus is the worst rickettsial disease. Typhus has killed millions of people and affected history in many ways. For example, typhus killed more than 150,000 of Napoleon's soldiers during his march on Moscow in 1812, contributing significantly to the defeat of the French invaders.

Typhus is transmitted from person to person by the body louse. If the louse bites an infected person, the rickettsias travel to its intestinal cells, which become infected and eventually break open, releasing rickettsias into the gut. They pass out with the feces, which can easily be scratched into the skin by the louse's itching human host. A week or two later, the infected person feels chills, fever, headaches, and aches and pains. A rash appears, too, and the victim is very seriously ill for two or three weeks. Without treatment, one in five patients dies from epidemic typhus. Fortunately, the disease can be treated with antibiotics, and epidemics can be avoided by public health measures such as vaccinations and elimination of lice.

Several other less common but often serious diseases are also caused by rickettsias. Rocky Mountain spotted fever and

Q fever are both carried by ticks. Despite its name, Rocky Mountain spotted fever is found in almost every state in the Union. Humans are infected by a tick bite and develop a rash, high fever, and terrific headache. Many victims die if untreated. Q fever is actually a disease transmitted by ticks to sheep, goats, and cattle. Humans can contract the disease, however, by breathing infected dust or drinking unpasteurized infected milk.

Venereal Diseases

Some bacteria die very quickly when exposed to air. Disease-causing bacteria which are this sensitive can successfully infect a new host only if they are passed from one individual to another with little or no exposure to air. The venereal diseases, which infect the sexual organs, belong to this group. Because they die so quickly when exposed to oxygen, such bacteria rarely infect a person except from sexual contact with someone who is infected. In the United States today, only the "common cold" is more common than the two chief venereal diseases, syphilis and gonorrhea. Both diseases, as well as three other uncommon venereal diseases, are caused by bacteria. Although syphilis and gonorrhea are easily treated with antibiotics, infected persons often do not see their doctors. Venereal diseases are not considered socially "acceptable" infections. Often the victim does not feel particularily ill. But despite the often minor symptoms, both syphilis and gonorrhea can result in very serious damage to the body.

Syphilis is caused by a minute spirochaete. The first sign of the disease, a painless sore called a chancre, appears as long as three months after infection. In women, the chancre may be in the vagina where it can't even be seen. Treated or not, the chancre eventually heals over.

Some time later, other symptoms appear. The spirochaetes have spread throughout the body, and sores, a rash, enlarged glands, and flulike symptoms may occur. These, too, can disappear without treatment. But this doesn't mean the disease is cured. Some victims never have any further sign of the disease, but others suffer relapses of the same symptoms or more severe ones as late as 30 years after contracting the disease. Damage to bones, the heart, and brain are common. The optic nerve may be damaged, blinding the victim. Women with syphilis may infect their babies, causing severe scarring, blindness, deafness, bone damage, and other serious problems. Many infected babies die.

Gonorrhea may be the most common of all venereal diseases. In fact, it is the most commonly reported of all infectious diseases, and some experts think that only one in nine cases of gonorrhea is even reported at all. Since women may have the disease without any visible symptoms, gonorrhea is especially difficult to eliminate. Even without symptoms, however, the disease can cause permanent damage to the reproductive system, preventing the woman from ever bearing children. While some men have no symptoms from gonorrhea, most have a white discharge from the penis and pain when urinating. Men, too, can be sterilized by gonorrhea, and blindness can result in a baby born from an infected mother.

Both syphilis and gonorrhea can be diagnosed and in many cases cured with little bother to the infected person, although gonorrhea bacteria are becoming increasingly resistant to antibiotics. The increased sexual activity of young people in recent years has led to a tremendous increase in the frequency of venereal disease, especially of gonorrhea. It is very important for people to realize that, even if they don't feel especially sick, they may be suffering from one of these illnesses and may end up with permanent damage to their bodies if they do not get treatment.

Food Poisoning

The various kinds of food poisoning caused by bacteria are examples of illness caused by the effects of toxins made by bacteria. The term "food poisoning" is used by people to cover a variety of painful intestinal diseases, from the agonizing but short-lived kind to the often fatal disease called botulism. Botulism is caused by a bacterium which can grow only in the absence of oxygen. It also cannot tolerate acid conditions. If nonacid food is not heated enough during the process of canning, all the dangerous bacteria may not be killed. Conditions within a can of meat or vegetables, for example, are perfect for the growth of these bacteria. There is no oxygen present, and there is plenty of nourishment.

As the bacteria grow, they produce poisons which affect the nervous system and are among the most potent toxins known. Just the slightest bit of them can cause serious illness or death. The victim has difficulty swallowing and breathing, gets double vision and paralysis of the arms and legs. Because of the danger of botulism, home canning of meat and vegetables, except acid foods such as tomatoes and pickled vegetables, must be done in a pressure cooker where it gets hot enough to kill the resistant spores of the bacteria. Because these bacteria produce gas as they grow, any jar or can of meat or vegetables which has lost its seal or is bulging is suspect and *should not even be tasted.*

Other kinds of food poisoning are not as serious, but they can be agonizingly painful while they last. The most common type is caused by a bacterium called *Staphylococcus aureus.* The genus name "Staphylococcus" comes from the Greek word *staphyle,* meaning "a bunch of grapes"; these bacteria tend to occur in clusters. The species name "aureus" was given because colonies grown on artificial media have a golden (*aureus* in Latin) color. At any one time, from 20 per cent to 75 per cent of persons have *Staphylococcus aureus* living somewhere on or in their bodies. Usually the bacteria cause no trouble. But if they get into food which is left out for a few hours before serving, such as cold meat, milk, or pastry, they can multiply rapidly, forming a toxin as they grow. People who eat the contaminated food suffer diarrhea and/or vomiting within a few hours. They may even get sick enough to require hospitalization, but within 24 hours the siege is over.

Staphylococcus can cause a variety of other diseases as well. In hospitals, where there are many people with lowered defenses against infection, outbreaks of staph disease can occur, resulting in infections of the skin, intestine, or lungs.

Body Defenses

By now you're probably wondering why you are ever healthy. Fortunately, the body has many ways to defend itself against disease-causing microorganisms. Although we inhale bacteria every time we breathe, our air passages are usually almost free of them. All our air passages, from the small bronchi in the lungs to the larger bronchi, trachea, larynx, and throat are lined with constantly beating cilia, much like those on ciliated protozoans. These cilia constantly carry a blanket of sticky mucus outward from the lungs and upward to the mouth. Bacteria and other small particles become trapped in the mucus and are carried to the mouth, where they are mixed with saliva and swallowed. Most swallowed bacteria perish in the strong hydrochloric acid of the stomach.

If bacteria should invade the body, they may be attacked

by macrophages and killed. Other cells in the immune system react to invading "germs" by producing special proteins called antibodies. The antibodies become attached to the bacterial cell wall and make it harmless. Antibodies are very specific; each kind can attach to only one kind of pathogen. When a pathogen invades for the first time, it takes a while for antibody-forming cells to begin production of the new sorts of antibodies necessary to fight it off. But the second time around, cells already present in the body can produce the now familiar antibodies very quickly. This is why particular diseases usually can make you sick only once. After you get the chicken pox, you don't have to worry about getting it again. Your body has "learned" how to fight off that particular disease.

The study of body defenses against disease is fascinating, but also very complex; many different kinds of body cells are involved in immunity, and we still have much to learn about it.

Nine

Where Did "Higher" Cells Come From?

Despite the great diversity of life on earth, all living things can be conveniently placed in one of two very distinct categories, prokaryotes and eukaryotes. No living thing has cells intermediate between these two different types. Yet, despite this clear division, all organisms are certainly related to one another. All use the same basic "genetic code" utilizing DNA to direct the development and function of their cells; and all cells have basically the same machinery, including ribosomes, for the manufacture of vital cell proteins.

Since prokaryotic cells are simpler and more ancient than eukaryotic cells, these must have evolved from their more primitive prokaryotic relatives. How did this transformation take place? This question has puzzled biologists and generated arguments among them for a long time. But as more and more is learned about cell structure and biochemistry, one particular theory gains increasing support among scientists —that eukaryotic cells arose from symbiosis between different kinds of prokaryotic cells.

To many biologists, this seems to be a far-fetched idea, but even some scientists are often unaware of the tremendous variety of symbioses which exist between cells in the living world today. Symbiosis of bacteria, algae, and fungi with eukaryotic cells is found all around us. Fascinating though it may be, there is nothing unusual about it. Even bare chloroplasts, stripped of their surrounding cytoplasm, thrive within the cells of certain sea slugs, carrying on normal photosynthesis there for weeks without the benefit of direction from their original plant cells. In this book we have investigated bacteria which live inside protozoa, insects, and plant cells. We have seen that the hosts often cannot survive without their prokaryotic guests. Such dependence can be established in an incredibly short span of time, with a laboratory strain of amoeba becoming dependent on an originally pathogenic kind of bacteria in a mere six years.

The Symbiotic Theory

During past decades, now and then some biologist would come up with the idea that mitochondria and sometimes chloroplasts resulted from symbiosis of bacteria with other cells. No one paid much attention to the idea until the 1960s, however, when sensitive biochemical methods and electron-microscope research allowed the careful study of mitochondria and chloroplasts. An especially exciting discovery was the presence of DNA within these organelles, or "little organs," for it had been assumed that all the DNA was inside the cell nucleus. Electron-microscope studies showed that chloroplasts and mitochondria contained their own protein-producers, or ribosomes, too, and soon it was learned that both organelles carried on protein-making under the direction of their own DNA, using their own ribosomes. These indications that mitochondria and chloroplasts had considerable independence from the cell nucleus revived the theory that they developed, many millions of years ago, from free-living bacteria.

Dr. Lynn Margulis has done more than any other biologist toward promoting and explaining the symbiotic theory. Her 1970 book, *Origin of Eukaryotic Cells,* has inspired innumerable arguments and experiments. Here is a quick summary of Dr. Margulis' theory. Several billion years ago, prokaryotic cells arose (how this happened is another story). They survived, grew, and multiplied by metabolizing energy-rich chemicals which were abundant in the waters of the early earth. The air nowadays consists of about 78 per cent nitrogen and 21 per cent oxygen, with about 1 per cent carbon dioxide and minute amounts of other gases. But billions of years ago, there was no free oxygen in the air. There was lots of ammonia and methane instead; the oxygen present on earth was locked up in water and in minerals.

Eventually some prokaryotes evolved the ability to use the sun's energy instead of relying on energy-containing compounds in the water. The first kinds of photosynthesis were somewhat primitive and did not release oxygen. Some bacteria today still use these relatively inefficient forms of photosynthesis. Later on, however, some prokaryotes became able to split water molecules into hydrogen and oxygen, combining the hydrogen with carbon dioxide to make sugars and releasing the oxygen into the air as a gas. This new development had important consequences for all cells, for, basically, oxygen is a potent cell poison, even though we are used to thinking of it as an important necessity for life. As the oxygen content of the air increased over millions of years from the activities of photosynthetic prokaryotes, other kinds had to adjust to the changes. Some retreated into the few remaining anaerobic habitats, such as dense mud, where their descendents are found today. But others evolved ways of dealing with the poisonous oxygen so they could survive in its presence.

A small cell has a harder time keeping oxygen out than does a large one. Perhaps some early prokaryotes evolved larger cells that could keep out oxygen; at this point we can only guess at the sequence of events leading up to eukaryote cells. The ability to move rapidly away from dangerously high concentrations of oxygen would also be a great advantage.

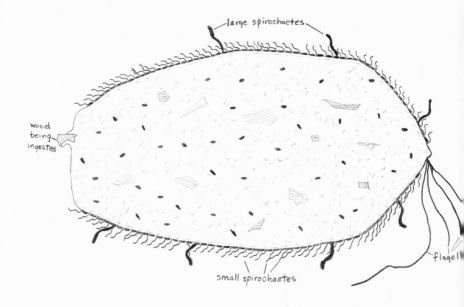

The protozoan Myxotricha is unique in that it moves about by the rotation of thousands of tiny spirochaetes attached to its outside surface. Some biologists believe that the flagella of modern organisms evolved from just this sort of association. Myxotricha also carries around rod-shaped bacteria and a few large spirochaetes attached to its outer surface. Inside, still different bacteria probably aid Myxotricha in digesting the wood particles it ingests at its amoeba-like back end. The individual shown here is in the process of ingesting a wood particle. The four flagella, which help Myxotricha steer, can be seen at the front end. DRAWING BY THE AUTHOR

Perhaps the first symbiosis to develop in these far-off times was between a large prokaryote and a moving one such as present-day spirochaetes, similar in nature to the symbiosis of spirochaetes with Myxotricha in the termite gut.

Theory says that the plasma membrane of this organism also became altered, allowing it to engulf its smaller "cousins" as food, much the same way as do modern amoebas. Such an organism would have many advantages over smaller, less mobile ones which were still dependent on dissolved nutrients in the water. Its larger size helped protect it against poisonous oxygen, and its mobility enabled it to escape from high oxygen concentrations. Its ability to engulf smaller organisms gave it a reliable source of concentrated food. We can imagine that such an organism was quite successful.

Other early prokaryotes had different ways of coping with oxygen. Although it is a poison, oxygen also has the potential of increasing the efficiency of metabolism greatly. Some bacteria evolved ways of using oxygen to help them extract more energy from their "food." These bacteria were also able to thrive, for oxygen didn't bother them and their metabolism was especially efficient.

In the process of engulfing food, our large oxygen-tolerant creature could be expected to have taken in some of the small oxygen-using prokaryotes. And since we know that bacteria can easily establish themselves inside cells, it is not hard to imagine that some of these early prokaryotes did just that. They had a way of resisting digestion and came to reside as symbionts inside the larger cells. They thus became established in a protected environment, and their hosts benefited from their special efficiency of energy transformations. Over the millions of years of evolution which followed, these symbionts became the mitochondria of modern eukaryotic cells. Chloroplasts came about in much the same way, according to this theory. Photosynthetic prokaryotes were engulfed but not digested and, over time, evolved into chloroplasts.

While quite a few biologists side with Dr. Margulis on the symbiotic origin of mitochondria and chloroplasts, fewer agree with her that flagella and cilia, as well as some other very important parts of the eukaryotic cell, developed from symbiotic spirochaetes that enabled the eukaryote ancestor to move about.

Mitochondria as Bacteria

The longer biochemists and other scientists have studied mitochondria, the more like bacteria they have appeared to be. The DNA in mitochondria is arranged in a circular strand like bacterial DNA, not into separate chromosomes like DNA in the eukaryote nucleus. The ribosomes in mitochondria resemble bacterial ribosomes more closely than they resemble the ribosomes in eukaryote cytoplasm. Protein-manufacture in bacteria and mitochondria is similar, and differs from that in the eukaryote cytoplasm.

Mitochondria are very specialized organelles that carry a series of enzymes that help to break down sugars, releasing energy to the cell. When these enzymes are studied, they turn out to be very similar to those found in various bacteria. One kind of bacteria, called *Paracoccus denitrificans,* is especially remarkable in its many similarities to mitochondria. Its membranes have many of the same building blocks as do those of mitochondria, and its enzymes are very similar to those of mitochondria. It is remarkable that, after so many millions of years of evolution, a bacterium which has so many similarities to mitochondria is still around.

We also find today an example of symbiosis which could serve as the model for an early stage in the evolution of mitochondria. The primitive amoeba Pelomyxa lacks several features of typical eukaryote cells, including mitochondria. But Pelomyxa always carries around a healthy population of symbiotic bacteria. The bacteria are surrounded by cell walls and exist inside spheres of membrane produced by the amoeba, so they are not as closely associated with it as mitochondria are with eukaryotic cells. But even so, they may serve a vital function to the amoeba. The amoeba cannot live long without oxygen, even though it can metabolize food without it. Scientists believe that the bacteria may help the amoeba by metabolizing its wastes, such as lactic acid, so they do not accumulate enough to kill it.

This may have been the original function of the prokaryotes which evolved into mitochondria. Perhaps only later, with loss of the cell wall and changes in the surrounding membrane, did they begin to provide energy to their hosts. As they lost their independence and became more and more important as energy-producers for the cell, their other functions became less important. They lost many unnecessary enzymes not concerned with releasing energy. Their membranes, where energy-production took place, became folded within; there was thus more surface area of membrane present, and this increased their efficiency. Some living bacteria have similar folds in their plasma membranes, though it is less extensive than those of mitochondria. But since the mitochondria have become increasingly specialized and more dependent on the eukaryotic cells for their other needs, they can devote more of their internal space to the energy-producing membranes.

Where Did Plants Come From?

Chloroplasts have greater independence than do mitochondria. They contain more DNA, so they manufacture more of their own proteins. Like the DNA of mitochondria, chloroplast DNA is organized like bacterial DNA, not like that from plants, and their ribosomes are also similar.

There is one big problem, however, in theorizing that chloroplasts evolved from symbiotic blue-green bacteria. Besides familiar green plants, there are several other types of plants, all called algae, which differ significantly in their types of chloroplasts. The structure of chloroplasts varies, and the kinds of chlorophyll involved in photosynthesis are different, too. Green algae and familiar green plants contain pigments called chlorophyll a and chlorophyll b, while brown algae, golden algae, and two other groups have chlorophyll a and chlorophyll c. Cyanobacteria and red algae have chlorophyll a and another different group of chemicals called phycobilins.

Because of these differences, Dr. Peter Raven has speculated that modern plants arose from symbioses of three different kinds of prokaryotes with early eukaryotes. He "invented" two kinds of prokaryotes which, he thought, were now extinct. One was a green one with chlorophylls a and b, which became symbiotic, giving rise to green plants. The other was a yellow one with chlorophylls a and c. Its symbioses gave rise, he said, to those algae with chlorophylls a and c. An early kind of blue-green bacteria became symbiotic to produce red algae.

Indeed, the resemblance between chloroplasts of certain single-celled red algae and cyanobacteria is striking. The folded membranes which almost fill the cell interior of Aphanocapsa (a single-celled cyanobacterium) look just like the chloroplast membranes of a red alga. Both red algae and cyanobacteria also share other characteristics, such as a unique way of gathering light, a common mechanism for capturing and transferring energy, and a very similar set of vital proteins involved in photosynthesis.

There is even a present-day organism, named *Cyanophora paradoxa,* which could easily represent an intermediate stage in the development of red algae. Cyanophora represents a symbiosis between a eukaryote and a prokaryote so closely that biologists had a hard time deciding if it was an alga or a combination of a colorless alga and a bacterium. In its cytoplasm, Cyanophora has structures which look just like chloroplasts with a light microscope. But with an electron microscope, a very reduced but definite cell wall can be seen surrounding the "chloroplasts." Thus they are not chloroplasts but are bacteria instead. The bacteria and the alga cannot survive without one another. It appears that the eukaryotic part of this symbiosis makes some vital contribution to chlorophyll synthesis as well as to other aspects of the bacteria's metabolism. The algal cell depends on the bacteria for photosynthesis. The two organisms are almost as thoroughly integrated with one another as are chloroplasts and plant cells.

Dr. Raven had to invent two kinds of prokaryotes as chloroplast ancestors because blue-green bacteria are just too different from most chloroplasts. His ideas have been criticized for this reason, for he had no way of proving that his invented ancestors ever lived. However, in 1977 a new kind of "algae" was found living as a symbiont with certain sea squirts in tropical parts of the Pacific Ocean. This organism is like green plants in that it possesses chlorophyll a and chlorophyll b. Instead of chloroplasts, it has photosynthetic membranes in the cytoplasm which are like those found in green alga chloroplasts. But, like cyanobacteria, it has no clear-cut nucleus. Here is a living "green prokaryote," like the one Dr. Raven had to invent as an ancestor to green plant chloroplasts. This exciting find greatly strengthens the symbiotic theory for chloroplast origins.

More Criticism

Not all biologists are happy with the symbiotic theory. They find it hard to believe that such completely integrated cell organelles as mitochondria and chloroplasts could have evolved from completely independent microorganisms. They point to the fact that many of the traits of mitochondria are controlled by the cell nucleus. Some chloroplast traits are controlled by the nucleus, too. How could the genetic control of these traits have been transferred from the organelles to the nucleus? We can see the beginnings of such "takeover" by the eukaryotic nucleus in some cases of symbiosis. Kappa particles, now known to be bacteria, can survive in only some strains of Paramecium. These strains have a particular genetic trait (gene) which controls the ability of Kappa to survive within them. This gene probably controls production of some substance which allows Kappa to survive.

Many millions of years have gone by since the symbioses leading to mitochondria and chloroplasts would have begun. Although the mechanism of genetic transfer from organelle to nucleus is not understood, plenty of time would have passed for such changes to occur. Chloroplasts and mitochondria have very specialized functions. As they became more efficient at these functions and more dependent on their host cells over periods of time, more and more of their internal spaces would have been devoted to doing their jobs; less and less space was devoted to carrying on functions which the rest of the host cell could perform equally well. The genetic information concerned with such functions would gradually be lost.

Altogether, it is easier to propose that present-day bacteria, mitochondria, and chloroplasts have similar or identical ancestors than to imagine that their shared traits were evolved independently. Why should mitochondria and chloroplasts, for example, evolve ribosomes more similar to those of bacteria than to those in the cytoplasm of the cells which contain them? Why should their enzymes be more similar to those of bacteria unless they are related to bacteria? The list of similarities is long, and the differences are of the type expected from the long evolution of a close, dependent relationship. As more and more is learned about cell organelles and bacteria, the evidence for the symbiotic theory will be either strengthened or weakened. Now, however, more and more biologists are accepting this exciting idea of how our complex and efficient cells came into being. If the symbiotic theory is correct, then symbiosis in one of the most basic properties of living cells.

Ten

Pushing into the Unknown
and Uncertain

Bacteria have been used by humans in many ways for generations. The famous holes in Swiss cheese are formed by carbon dioxide gas released by bacteria while they are in the process of altering milk to turn it into cheese, and it is bacteria that turn wine into vinegar. Old-fashioned dill pickles and sauerkraut are other products which result from the harnessing of bacterial fermentation for human use.

Modern-day scientists use bacteria for many vital studies of biological problems, from evolution to biochemistry. Culturing them in the laboratory is a simple process. Since some species divide every 20 minutes, countless numbers can be produced overnight. Much of our knowledge of cell function comes from studies of the prokaryotic cell, because it is simpler than the eukaryotic cell and because it can be cultured so easily in such large numbers. As knowledge of the way bacterial cells function increases, researchers look more and more toward ways of making these microorganisms work for humans. A sampling of recent research will give some idea of how useful these minute cells can be.

Living Solar Batteries

We've seen that some bacteria are adapted to living in challenging environments. A very unusual species found in waters with high salt concentration, called Halobacterium, is being investigated as a possible source of efficient solar energy. This organism has a purplish-red pigment called bacteriorhodopsin, which can generate electricity directly from sunlight. Photosynthetic systems with chlorophyll use a complicated series of 30 or more enzymes to produce a stream of electrons. These electrons could conceivably be trapped and made to flow through a wire as an electric current. The system is so complicated that it would be difficult to harness. But Halobacterium uses only one enzyme to extract energy from sunlight. Already, Lester Packer of the Lawrence Berkeley Laboratory has used bacteriorhodopsin to produce electricity, enough to light up a very small light bulb for 90 minutes.

If bacteriorhodopsin can be harnessed in a practical way, it could be helpful in solar-energy collection, but it would have other uses as well. In the bacteria, the pigment functions to pump positively charged ions out of the cell. This property could be exploited to remove salt from sea water for use in countries by the sea which have little fresh water. It might also be used to concentrate valuable minerals or toxic chemicals from oceans, lakes, or sewage.

The round blobs are colonies of billions of fire blight bacteria growing on the surface of a jelled nutrient medium. This is one way in which bacteria are grown for scientific study. SHERMAN V. THOMSON

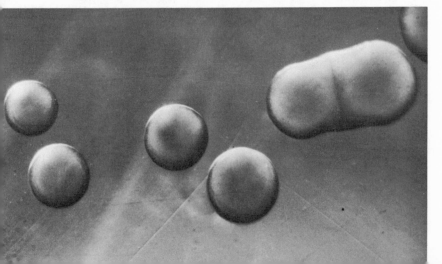

Infecting Pests

Animals besides humans have diseases, some of which kill. In recent years biologists have begun to develop some of the diseases of pests into forms which make them usable in pest control. The bacterium *Bacillus thuringensis* kills caterpillars of many butterflies and moths, and "cabbage worms" (butterfly larvae) and tomato and tobacco hornworms (moth caterpillars) are serious crop pests. Farmers and gardeners can buy a powder containing spores of this bacterium. The spores have crystals which are lethal to caterpillars and can also infect the animals with a fatal disease. Unlike many pesticides, the bacteria cause absolutely no harm to plants or to other animals, and their cost is reasonable.

In 1978, another bacterium was found to be fatal to mosquitos. Just a single dose of bacterial spores in the water and, within 18 hours, almost all the mosquito larvae were dead. The rest died later. The disease affects only mosquitos and, if all goes well, it may become available for purchase in the United States by 1981. It is probably the most efficient mosquito-killer ever developed.

Possibilities with Nitrogen Fixation

Human hunger is an extremely compelling problem today, and a large part of the difficulty in producing enough food is the lack of sufficient fixed nitrogen to grow abundant crops in much of the world. One important project is to survey more species of legumes to see which are nodulated; so far only about 10 per cent of the more than 10,000 species of plants in the family have even been examined to see if they are nodulated. Fewer than 50 legume species are presently grown in cultivation; maybe others presently growing wild could become crop plants, too.

Scientists are working now on the possibilities of developing partnerships between grain crops and nitrogen-fixing bacteria. In one experimental plot, some corn plants growing in nitrogen-deficient soil were noticed which were larger than their neighbors. Nitrogen-fixing bacteria were found associated with their roots, so biologists are hopeful that strains of corn or wheat can be developed which would attract nitrogen-fixers. Plant varieties with roots which released carbon-rich chemicals into the soil could be selected, and bacteria capable of using those chemicals and of fixing nitrogen could be teamed up with the grains.

Biologists are also trying to develop strains of nitrogen-fixers which are more efficient. Bacteria are exposed to agents, such as radiation, which alter their genetic structure, and the resulting cells are cultured. One such experiment resulted in bacteria which produced twice as many nodules as ordinary strains and which resulted in plants which have about twice as much fixed nitrogen as ordinary plants. Only time will tell, however, if such laboratory-grown strains could compete with the natural kinds found in the soil in fields.

Fooling Nature

Fixing nitrogen costs energy, and organisms invest that energy only when they have to. If legumes are planted in nitrogen-rich soil, few nodules will develop and the plants will fix little nitrogen. After all, there is already plenty there. Biologists are working on developing bacteria which will fix nitrogen continuously, regardless of the amount of nitrogen in the surrounding soil. Mutant strains of one free-living nitrogen-fixer now exist which continue to fix nitrogen and even release ammonia in the presence of fertilizer. Perhaps these bacteria could be grown in ponds on a cheap waste material such as paper-mill wastes, turning junk into valuable fertilizer. It would be even more exciting if ammonia-excreting strains of blue-green bacteria could be developed. These could be grown in ordinary ponds, without need for any added energy source, and the pond contents could be harvested as fertilizer.

Other scientists are working on ways to bypass the bacteria altogether and develop plants which can fix nitrogen by themselves. In order to do this, the genes from bacteria which control nitrogenase and its production would have to be transferred directly into plant cells and incorporated into their genetic systems. This is no easy matter, but the possibilities are there. One problem lies with the ribosomes. Since bacterial ribosomes are different from plant ones, the plant ribosomes might have trouble translating information from bacterial genes. Perhaps the genes could be introduced into plant mitochondria or chloroplasts, where the ribosomes are more similar to bacterial ones than are those in the cytoplasm.

There is some evidence, however, that a natural system exists in which bacterial genes are actually transferred into plant cells and able to function there. Strangely enough, plants can get a kind of cancer. It is called "crown gall disease." Tumors grow near the crown of the plant, the region where the root and stem meet. The disease is transmitted to plants by a bacterium named Agrobacterium. After years of study and controversy, it now appears that the bacteria transfer circular pieces of DNA, called plasmids, into the plant cells. The plasmids induce into the plant cells such characteristics as uncontrolled growth. If plasmids can transfer undesirable traits into plants, perhaps they could be induced to transfer desirable ones as well, such as the ability to fix nitrogen.

Scientists are also trying to figure out ways to transfer

This pecan tree suffers from crown gall disease. Wartlike growths from a few inches to a foot or more in diameter form on the base of a tree trunk and larger roots. USDA

plasmids into animal cells and get the plasmids to function there. If this could be accomplished, it might be possible to correct genetic diseases, such as hemophilia, by making plasmids carry correct genes into cells to replace the faulty inherited ones.

Problems, Problems

There are many difficulties with transferring genes from prokaryotes into eukaryotes. Because of the very different organization of the chromosomes, eukaryotic cells might have trouble translating bacterial genes even if they were successfully introduced. The genes also would have to be copied and passed on whenever the plant or animal cells divided during growth; this could also be a big problem. Other technical problems exist as well, but the great promise that these techniques would offer for agriculture and medicine spurs scientists on toward solving the difficulties.

Some people feel that the techniques used in these "genetic engineering" experiments are dangerous. They fear that in the process of mixing DNA from different species, hazardous bacteria could result which might cause terrible epidemics or perhaps induce cancer. Because of these concerns, special regulations must be followed in laboratories receiving government money for this type of research. As more and more of these experiments are carried out with no sign of any potential problems, biologists worry less about the accidental production of a "supergerm."

Even if bacterial genes can be successfully introduced into eukaryotes, difficulties would still exist. For example, nitrogen-fixing cereals would have to devote considerable energy to the nitrogen-fixing process. They would yield less per acre than do present, artificially fertilized strains. Also, the energy drain would probably result in slower growth, so the new kinds would take longer to reach maturity and could not be grown as far north or south as present varieties can. In time, if nitrogen was no longer the limiting factor in crop production, another mineral would eventually become limiting. Perhaps it would be one of the other major minerals, such as potassium or phorphorus. Or it could be a trace element such as molybdenum.

Oil-Eaters

Plasmids can also be used to transfer genes from one strain of bacteria into another. This is much simpler than introducing bacterial genes into eukaryotic cells, and already scientists are working hard on modifying bacteria to suit human needs. One good example of this technique is the development of bacteria which may be able to "eat" oil slicks at sea. When oil tankers run aground and leak oil, ecological disaster results. The tanker *Torrey Canyon* released about 100,000 tons of crude oil into the English Channel, and the *Metula* spilled 50,000 tons into Antarctic waters rich in marine life. The *Metula* slick covered 1000 square miles of the sea and coated 75 miles of the Chilean coastline with black, choking oil. No one knows how many marine creatures lost their lives in these and other such disasters.

Bacteria which break down oil chemicals live naturally in the sea. But they aren't found in the large numbers necessary to break up a slick, and each strain can handle only one or a few of the many complex molecules present in crude oil. One scientist developing superstrains of oil-eating bacteria is Dr. Ananda M. Chakrabarty at the General Electric Research and Development Center. Using genetic engineering, Dr. Chakrabarty put the genes of four different bacterial strains together to create a hybrid which can break down two-thirds of the chemicals in a slick. The waste products are proteins which can be consumed easily by other marine life. This sort of research is still so new that its eventual practical success cannot be predicted. Tests on real oil slicks, outside laboratories, must be done, and ways of releasing the bacteria on the slicks so that they can go to work in time must be developed. One hopes that some day soon bacteria will be put to work, breaking up oil spills before they harm the environment.

Bacterial Factories

Bacteria grown in large quantities already manufacture important substances such as the antibiotic streptomycin and medically useful enzymes. With the development of genetic engineering, using plasmids, researchers are enthusiastic about turning bacteria into factories for making many different useful substances. Protein hormones are very expensive to manufacture in a chemical laboratory, so when they are needed in large quantities, they are obtained from slaughterhouses.

Insulin is a very complicated protein, and it is vital in the treatment of diabetes. Animal insulins are now used for treatment of this common disease. Animal insulins are different from human insulin, and some doctors believe that some of the problems associated with diabetes are caused by long-term use of such foreign proteins. In 1978 biologists succeeded in coaxing bacteria to make human insulin in the laboratory. First the researchers put together two artificial genes, each of which coded for one of the two protein chains which make up the insulin molecule. The artificial genes were linked with a set of genes which the biologists knew how to regulate. This new genetic mixture was combined into plasmids, which transferred it into bacterial cells. Some bacteria were given the gene for one chain and others got the gene for the other chain. By "turning on" the set of genes which was added to the bacteria along with the insulin ones, the researchers were able to induce the bacteria to produce the insulin chains. Once they had the two pieces and had purified them, they put them together. A significant number (10 to 40 per cent) of the chains combined in the correct way, forming human insulin molecules.

Now researchers are figuring out ways to put the bacteria to work in a large-scale fashion so that enough insulin is made to sell profitably. It is only a matter of time before bacteria will be churning out insulin and other proteins which will benefit humans enormously. Bacteria have been helping plants and animals for countless generations. But we have just scratched the surface in harnessing the great potential which bacteria hold as helpers to humans in our modern world.

Glossary

aerobic: Able to live in the presence of oxygen.

algae (s., *alga*): A word used to cover various plantlike organisms popularly known as seaweeds; some algae have been classified with the protozoa in the Kingdom Protista.

anaerobic: Able to live in the absence of oxygen.

antibodies: Proteins (made by special cells in the body) that combine with foreign substances in the body; antibodies make invading bacteria and viruses inactive.

bacilli (s., *bacillus*): Rod-shaped bacteria.

bacteriophage: A virus that attacks bacteria.

blue-green algae: Organisms now generally accepted as being more closely related to bacteria than to algae; for this reason, they are preferably called blue-green bacteria or cyanobacteria.

cell: The smallest unit of independent life; all living things are made up of cells.

cell wall: A protective layer secreted outside the plasma membrane by bacteria, algae, and plants; bacterial and plant-cell walls are very different in chemical composition.

cellulose: The main component of plant-cell walls.

chlorophyll: A green chemical important in photosynthesis of plants, some bacteria, and some algae; there are several different forms of chlorophyll.

chloroplast: A cell organelle of algae and plants filled with membranes which contain chlorophyll and sometimes other photosynthetic pigments.

cilia (s., *cilium*): Short, often numerous cell organelles with quite complex structure; identical with flagella, but shorter.

cocci (s., *coccus*): Spherical bacteria.

commensal: An organism living with a different species that benefits from its association without harming its host.

crustaceans: Shrimps, crabs, and their relatives.

cyanobacteria: Another name for blue-green bacteria.

cytoplasm: The fluid portion of the cell outside the nucleus.

DNA: The chemical within cells, mostly in the nucleus, which carries the genetic information.

enzyme: A protein which aids in carrying out a particular chemical reaction or set of similar reactions in the cell.

eukaryote: An organism with a definite nucleus, surrounded by a membrane and containing chromosomes visible when the cell divides; and mitochondria, organelles which carry on the metabolic reactions releasing energy for use by the cell. Some eukaryotes also have chloroplasts.

feces: The waste material of the digestive tract, released through the anus.

fermentation: A chemical process for breakdown of energy-containing substances, such as sugars, which does not use free oxygen.

flagella (s., *flagellum*): Cell organelles which move, often functioning to propel a small organism through the water. There are two kinds of flagella: the bacterial type is thin, simple, and probably functions by rotating; the eukaryotic type is much larger, has complex structure, and beats in a whiplike fashion.

gene: The unit of heredity. It consists of a particular section of a chromosome or of a DNA molecule and controls some process or trait.

legume: A plant belonging to the large family Leguminosae, which includes peas, beans, clover, and acacias. The roots of many legumes have lumps called nodules which contain nitrogen-fixing bacteria.

metabolism: The complex chemical activities of an organism that provide energy and tissue components from the food taken in.

mitochondria (s., *mitochondrion*): Microscopic cell organelles that produce energy for eukaryotic cells, a process that requires oxygen.

mycetocyte: A cell within the body of an organism such as an insect, that contains symbionts, often bacteria.

mycetome: A specialized organ of the body of an organism such as an insect, that contains mycetocytes.

nitrogen fixation: The chemical reaction of atmospheric nitrogen (N_2) that produces ammonia. Only some bacteria are able to fix nitrogen; plants and animals cannot use atmospheric nitrogen.

nitrogenase: The enzyme which enables some bacteria to fix nitrogen; nitrogenase will only function in the absence of oxygen.

nucleus (pl., *nuclei*): The part of the eukarytoic cell, separated from the rest of the cell by a membrane, that contains most of the genetic information in chromosomes.

organelle: A specialized part of the cell, such as a mitochondrion or flagellum, that carries out a particular cell function; in effect, a "little organ" of a cell.

parasite: An organism which lives in or on another to obtain its nutrition, causing some degree of harm to its host.

pathogen: A disease-causing organism.

photosynthesis: The process by which plants, some protista, and some bacteria are able to harness the sun's energy to produce energy-rich compounds such as sugars.

plaque: Surface film of material on teeth, consisting largely of bacteria, which can lead to cavity formation.

plasma membrane: The thin membrane surrounding a cell; also called the cell membrane.

plasmid: Small circle of DNA carrying various genes which can be transferred into a cell.

prokaryote: An organism with simple cells lacking mitochondria, chloroplasts, and a defined nucleus with chromosomes; bacteria, including those often incorrectly called blue-green algae, are prokaryotes.

protein: Chemical consisting of a long chain of hundreds or thousands of building blocks called amino acids. The molecule may be very large, and the chain may be twisted into a complex three-dimensional shape; proteins are vital to living things as enzymes, structural chemicals, etc.

protist: An organism belonging to the Kingdom Protista, which consists of the protozoa and most algae.

protozoa (s., *protozoan;* also *protozoon*): Usually single-celled organisms once considered to belong to the animal kingdom but now placed in a separate kingdom, the Protista, by most biologists.

Rhizobium: A species of bacteria that cause legume roots to form nodules.

rhizosphere: An area around the roots within which roots have an effect on other living things in the soil.

ribosome: A small cell organelle in which proteins are made. Prokaryotes and eukaryotes have ribosomes that are somewhat different from each other.

rumen: The large first chamber of the ruminant stomach.

ruminant: An animal that has a rumen, such as a cow, sheep, or camel.

spirochaete: A spiral-shaped bacterium with peculiar structure; flagella are attached near the ends of the cell and extend toward the opposite end; the entire cell, including the flagella, is surrounded by a membrane.

symbiont: A partner in symbiosis.

symbiosis: The living together of different species of organisms. In this book the term does not imply any particular benefit from the relationship, but it is often used in that way.

virus: A minute particle, consisting of a central core of nucleic acid and a surrounding protein coat, which can function only inside living cells; it takes over the cell machinery and makes it produce more virus particles.

Suggested Reading

Books

Michael Andrews, *The Life that Lives on Man* (Taplinger, N.Y., 1977). Tells about various symbionts on humans, including bacteria.

Peter Baldry, *The Battle Against Bacteria: A Fresh Look* (2nd ed., Cambridge University Press, N.Y., 1976). Gives the history of bacteriology, especially as related to human diseases.

Bernard Dixon, *Magnificant Microbes* (Atheneum, N.Y., 1976). Tells the uses of microbes and of our dependence on them.

Hans Zinsser, *Rats, Lice, and History* (Little, Boston, 1935). A classic study of the epidemic disease typhus.

Magazine Articles

Winston J. Brill, "Biological Nitrogen Fixation," *Scientific American*, March 1977

Eugenie Clark, "Flashlight Fish of the Red Sea," *National Geographic*, November 1978

Kim Cottrell, "Superstrain of Oil-Eating Microbes," *Sea Fronteirs*, Jan.–Feb. 1977

Audrey Glauert, "World Within a World," *Natural History*, Nov. 1962 (Structure of bacteria)

Gerald Keusch, "Ecology of the Intestinal Tract," *Natural History*, November 1974

Lynn Margulis, "Symbiosis and Evolution," *Scientific American*, August 1971 (Also available as Scientific American Offprint #1230.)

John E. McCosker, "Flashlight Fishes," *Scientific American*, March 1977

Ronald S. Oremland, "Microorganisms and Marine Ecology," *Sea Frontiers*, Sept.–Oct. 1976

Index